ORPHAN TALES
A Search for Truth, Love and Family

by

Nanette Davis

TELEMACHUS PRESS

ORPHAN TALES: A Search for Truth, Love and Family

Cover designed by Nanette Davis

Cover art:
Copyright © iStockPhotophoto_950157308_sankai

Published by Telemachus Press, LLC
7652 Sawmill Road
Suite 304
Dublin, Ohio 43016
http://www.telemachuspress.com

Visit the author website:
www.nanette-davis.com

ISBN: 978-1-948046-66-4 (eBook)
ISBN: 978-1-948046-67-1 (Paperback)
ISBN: 978-1-948046-79-4 (Hardback)

BIOGRAPHY & AUTOBIOGRAPHY/ Personal Memoirs

Version 2019.06.19

Dedication

This book is dedicated to Harriet Bressler Wolf, my mother, and to all of the gracious individuals in my family who have helped give me a second chance at life and to allow me to become the woman that I am today. You know who you are. Thank you for saving me.

… and without any regrets …

To the woman who so courageously endured nine months with a living daughter inside of her, and for having loved me enough to give me that second chance. May we meet again one day.

Author's Note

This a work of truth and of memory to the best that I can recall. All the family names used in this story are the actual names of the people they are intended to be. Several of the professionals' and the doctors' names have been changed to protect their privacy, but the positions that they hold are true.

My memoir was written to help other people like me. People who have not known their birth mothers, and have loved their adoptive mothers yet have suffered estrangement in their relationship, only to recapture that infinite bond years later.

It was suggested by my intuitive and caring Hospice counselor in 2008 that I write about my special relationship with my mother and how it shaped both of us. I am glad that I took her advice. I am a better person for it.

I always believed that there is a spiritual connection between mother and child. This begins at the very moment the egg has traveled on its long and miraculous journey settling in and buried deep into the sea of fluid and tissue that we call the womb. Something takes place in that warm, dark, and safe haven that none of us can see. Well, not initially. The umbilical cord remains the only physical evidence of that connection and *it*, in my opinion, is given to us because of our limited ability to see beyond the tangible.

I feel that every human being on this planet craves to know their origins. It is the true essence of who we are: to know our roots. This discussion has come up many times between my husband and me, but no one, no matter how loving, can truly understand this craving in its entirety, unless they are adopted and have lived a secret that is left untold for so long.

"The past is never fully gone. It is absorbed into the present and the future. It stays to shape what we are and what we do."

~Sir William Deane, Inaugural Lingiari Lecture, Darwin, 22, August 1996

ORPHAN TALES
A Search for Truth, Love and Family

Table of Contents

Acknowledgements

This story was conceived from my childhood and adult memory. Events are still unfolding on a monthly basis, and I am responding in kind to each dilemma and roadblock, as I tread through the muddy waters of birthright and identity.

I am forever grateful to those individuals who have been on this journey alongside me every day, and have been my support, both in positive and challenging times.

Extreme gratitude and love goes out to my beautiful, kind and loving cousin, Elaine Langsam. You watched me grow from a child into a woman, and have offered only encouragement, with your perpetual optimism. The world needs more strong women like you, and "living large" describes you completely. You will always be my north star.

Deepest gratitude and love goes out to my very dear friend, Betty Smith. I've been overwhelmed by your relentless encouragement, generosity, extreme wit and realistic attitude. Because of you, I've learned to take life as it comes, and that no matter what unfolds, it's usually "fantastic!" Thanks for listening to my writing rants, and for providing an excellent distraction through your culinary treasures, and wine inspired dinners.

I would be remiss if I didn't thank two special friends, Alec and Bennett Smith, who along with their wives, Jennifer and Ashleigh Smith, created my beautiful writing studio. The serene and functional space, was built with love and sweat equity. I can't thank each of you enough for your creativity and diligence. You've been, and will continue to be, a positive force in my life.

I want to thank my editor, Lynn Taylor. I believe you were sent to me by someone who knew that you were the woman for the job. I feel lucky to have met you, and to work with someone who fully understands my story and the desire to tell it. Your encouragement and patience has been nothing short of amazing, and I knew I could trust your judgement from the start of my book project. Thank you for allowing me the freedom to email you countless times with questions that seemed silly, but yet you treated every one of them with equal importance, as you knew it meant so much to me. I'm so glad to be going through this journey with you, and to have become your friend. Because of your kind words and professional help, I'm ready to move on to the next step.

Special thanks to all of my fellow scribes from the Keep St Pete Lit writing group and Lit Space classes. You helped me to begin a new phase in my writing, and to move forward in confidence and to write more. A special shout-out to Mike, Tracy, Patia, Julia, Gary, Tom, Lori, June, Bonnie and Lisa. You were the first people I met at Keep St Pete Lit, and walked the adoption memoir journey with me, even if it wasn't your genre. Thank you for all of your support and kind words of encouragement, or in some cases, much needed "opportunities for growth."

A big thank you to my friend and fellow scribe, Brit "Buster" Chism. You have been an inspiration for my writing since the first day we met at KSPL. I was mesmerized by your stories and interesting writing style from day one. Your honesty and no-nonsense approach to my writing, was exactly what I needed, especially early on, when I didn't know one comma from another. I consider myself fortunate to work with you, and more importantly, to have you as a friend. Thanks for the laughs.

A very special thanks to my cheerful and long-time friend, Kathy Pashkow, who had known me before all of this writing business started. You are the most positive person I know, and your continual support of my total self has been your goal. I can't thank you enough for pushing me harder in the gym, and insisting I could do more, improving both my body and mind, even though I complained routinely. Your dedication to what is good in life shows every single day, and you will always be part of my life.

Thank you to my friend, Tricia Christen-Rivas, who read this story in its infancy and devoted many hours to review an early manuscript, that was too embarrassing for public view. I appreciated all of the late nights you spent working with me, while simultaneously trying to run a successful business. Thank you for your continual support of my craft, and you have helped me in ways you can't imagine.

Some special thanks go out to my long-time friend, Jean, who heard this story, not as a manuscript, but as a conversation over many cups of coffee and countless boxes of tissues. You know more about me than my own family, and I trusted you from the beginning of our friendship. Thank you for caring about me, past, present and future, and for bringing a beautiful furry friend into my life.

I want to thank Steven Himes and MaryAnn Nocco, of Telemachus Press. You have been my guide throughout the publishing process, one that I was totally unfamiliar, and at times, overwhelmed with. I appreciate your willingness to engage me in my book project, and to offer valuable suggestions. I couldn't have asked for better assistance with technology, which is my nemesis, but you made it possible, and I'm grateful for your patience. Thank you for turning a childhood dream into a reality.

With deepest gratitude, and love to my husband, Robin Davis, who watched a woman, over thirty-three years, emerge into a serious writer, one who was willing to risk judgment, and ridicule for telling her true story. Thank you, dear Robin, for giving me the space, both physically and emotionally, to work long hours into the night, or wee hours in the morning, to complete my memoir. You endured doors slamming, occasional cussing, scanty dinners, all for the sake of "one more page." Even though you often said, "I know nothing about writing," your eyes spoke what you couldn't say, and your feedback has been invaluable. May we always be each other's best story.

And finally, to all adopted people around the globe, young and old. *Your* lives matter, every single day. You are a first class-citizen, and always have been, no matter what the outcome. You are true and real. You are here, and you are love.

Prologue

MONEY MAY HAVE exchanged hands the day I was born. If so, how much money was I worth, I wonder, to both parties? Was the amount negotiated, maybe even renegotiated?

It is strange to imagine that a frail and fragile newborn might be sold. Maybe the young woman from whose body I sprang to life felt that she needed the money. But her real reason for relinquishing custody of me on the very day of my birth remains unknown. I wonder if I was even suckled. Did I partake of at least that much of the woman who bore me? I have never been made privy to that information.

Perhaps the young woman lay desperately alone and frightened in a hospital room, without family or friends to comfort her. Once I found out about her, I wondered: Was she without a husband? Had my birthfather died, had he been married, or had he simply abandoned her? My God, could she have been raped? Am I the progeny of such a terrifying experience? I'll never know.

This much I do know. She has never been Mother to me. Mother is the woman who stood in the hospital corridor shuddering with excitement, her husband, my father, by her side. There they waited with open arms and open hearts to receive the infant they so desperately wanted.

How fortunate I am that they did not reject me. I can hardly fathom their reaction when they first saw me—a long, skinny, tow-headed blonde thing with chicken claw feet. But Harriet Bressler Wolf and Herman "Jack" Wolf, her husband through five long childless years, looked upon me with absolute awe. It was love at first sight.

Something else happened between the birthing room and that hospital corridor, something of which neither the abandoning mother nor the receiving mother was aware. It is this. I, the scrawny infant, was infused with my own soul. The spark took, the spirit was ignited. And the child, the young woman, the adult I would become, began to develop at that precise moment.

For more than 50 years, I never even knew the hospital-bed mother existed. I knew only what my parents wanted me to know. And so, during the final week of her life in 2008, my mother startled me with a blunt pronouncement. "I'm not your only mother," she screamed loudly from her death bed. Hospice nurses and nursing assistants responded to the screaming, looking quickly from my mother to me and back again. But they took no action. What could they do? So many questions, and no time left for answers from the one woman who could provide them.

A journey of renewed self-discovery began even as I mourned Mother's passing. The deepest corners of my heart have been turned inside out, laid bare, and the meaning of forgotten memories have been brought into the light. The soul that came to life on July 5, 1955 has now begun to heal, to be whole again. And in the process, this story has emerged.

A Stark Revelation

MY FATHER DIED on February 20, 1997 at ninety years of age, after my mother and I made what was deemed to be the *only* decision to disconnect him from his ventilator and tubes, without the traditional goodbyes. My father's sister, Aunt Mickey, and I were standing in front of the Boca Hospital while my mom was left with the awful "business" chores of death. She must have known I couldn't handle it then and dismissed both of us to the outside lobby area. It was at that precise moment that my life came to a screeching halt, which seemed to be in slow-motion, when Aunt Mickey glanced over at me and glibly blurted out, "Nanette, your father would be proud of you because you did so good for an adopted girl."

Having been unaware that I *was* adopted, the weight of that statement forced me to my knees right then and there, but the far-reaching effects of that truth extended long into my life. I forced myself to stand still as every muscle quivered deep inside my body. *Oh, my God,* I thought to myself. *Can this really be happening to me? Where did my life go? Who am I?* My heart was crying out. *I want my mommy, where's my mommy?* I felt like I was gasping for air, but I managed to breathe as I held onto the banister. Aunt Mickey was totally clueless that I never knew about my adoption, and I never mentioned to her that she had revealed a long-kept family secret.

Even though I was blindsided by the comment she made, it was a reaffirming moment for me of what I always knew in my heart of hearts. I always knew that something was not right with me as a little child. I possessed intense longing to know *everything* about *everyone* in my family at a young age while asking the "why" questions over and over again.

While most little girls spent their time playing with dolls or sporting their latest dress, I was off in a faraway place pondering my very existence. I studied every move and smile my mom made, searching endlessly for something, but not knowing what. I have been on that trail for truth for so many years that closure to this mystery would be welcomed.

Reaffirmation

SEVERAL DAYS HAD passed after Aunt Mickey dropped the adoption bomb on my doorstep, and Mom, Aunt Mickey, and I had come back to the house after the military funeral to sit "Shiva," a Jewish tradition following a funeral, although ours was less formal. The funeral itself was a blur as I sat in the first pew, still devastated and numbed by the words I heard days before. My reaction to my father's death was understated to say the least, and I barely can piece together memories of the internment that followed. Part of me mourned more for my mother, who had never known another relationship and would be left solo after forty plus years of marriage, and part of me celebrated the release of the overly strict father who gave love only when it suited him. There wasn't a soul at the service on that day, other than myself, who would have known how difficult things had been between us.

If this event had taken place in an Orthodox or Conservative Jewish home, all of the mirrors would have been covered, so mourners would not be concerned with their looks and more focused on the deceased. In addition, they would be sitting on small, hard stools so as to be reminded of the gravity of the situation and not to experience comfort.

A small group of family members, including much of my dad's side of the family, were present. The family was shrinking rapidly due to everyone's age. Stuart, my father's nephew and June, his niece, both twenty years older than me, were in attendance as well as a few of my mother's friends. As we sat and chatted about family life on Mom's enclosed porch, Aunt Mickey consoled my mother at the dining room table along with my mom's favorite cousin, Elaine. My thoughts turned once again to the moments in time only days before, of what I had learned in reference to being adopted. Even though several days had passed, the shock of hearing this information for the first time and being surrounded by supportive family after the funeral was almost too much to bear, but I kept my face devoid of all emotion as if nothing had happened and I was in full denial. My heart continued to sink, and my head felt like it was moving deeper into the abyss, and I was having difficulty concentrating. I felt alone even though I was surrounded by many people.

As we continued to chat for several hours on the porch away from mom and my aunt, the reaction of these kind relatives was one of mixed emotion. The surprise and the secrecy which surrounded this grand faux pas of Aunt Mickey's created an unwelcome commotion as we tried to grieve my father's death. Everyone appeared confused and bewildered at the fact that I was never *told* about my adoption.

My older cousin Stuart's reaction was one of complete shock and he responded by saying, "What does it really matter? *We are your family.* You don't need to know where you came from. Why would you want to know any differently?"

As it turned out, I learned that afternoon and evening from these relatives that everyone in my family and friends of the family all knew that I was adopted. I was the only individual who was not notified. Imagine that! This further created an atmosphere of uncertainty for me, as I plowed ahead later that day trying to keep up with the tempo of a saga right out of Peyton Place and I was the main event.

I held onto a secret of my own that night, as Mom knew nothing of what Aunt Mickey had revealed. I spoke very little to my aunt after my dad's death, as I felt she would be devastated about revealing a secret held for more than forty-seven years. She would have most likely insisted that I should discuss the matter with my mom, but that was out of the question. My mother had her reasons why she kept my adoption secret, and I believed that it was because she feared I would seek out another mother, and that she would vanish from my heart forever.

It was after seven o'clock that evening that I boarded the Southwest plane to head home, carrying a huge bag of food that my mom insisted that I take. Aunt Mickey was spending the next few nights with my mother, and I had gone back to St. Petersburg for an important appointment the next day. I vowed to be back within the week, although I felt guilty about leaving my mother alone without my father. Nonetheless, I jumped on that aircraft, tears flowing non-stop, as people were staring at me, wondering what had happened. The security agents at the Ft. Lauderdale airport ransacked my food, and I threw it all in the garbage, all the while bawling my eyes out letting them know it was from my mom's Shiva. They didn't care. Why should they?

Later that evening, back home in St. Petersburg, my husband Robin and I exchanged a few words about the service and what followed at Mom's house. I didn't have the energy to explain all of the details and promised to update him in the morning. I pulled off my funeral clothes and threw them in the hamper, vowing never to wear them again.

As I was half asleep in my own bed, Stuart's wife, Bonnie, graciously called to offer help and advice. She saw herself as the family counselor, as she was a licensed psychologist with a private practice. Although I did not have a close relationship with her at the time, I want to say that she reassured me that my adoption reveal was a big deal and would have to be dealt with at some point. We vowed to talk again on the subject, and I felt rescued by her calming words and the deep slumber that ensued shortly after our conversation.

Part One
The Early Years: Adopted Life Revisited

The Wooden Shoe
1959

I STOOD ON the steps of a building ten years ago that had terrified me when I was four years old. It was called the Wooden Shoe. The building looked exactly as I remembered it. Robin and I were taking a trip down memory lane through my old neighborhood in New York. I wanted to show him where I grew up and some of the memorable sights along the way.

At the time, my parents had moved into a small one-bedroom apartment while their house was being built on Long Island. All of the buildings were old brick with beautiful windows and overflowing gardens on all sides of the property. The grounds were manicured in the same way as they were in 1959.

In a corner structure amidst the garden apartments was a famous nursery school. It was well known in several towns adjacent to one another and was run by a kind woman named Mrs. Ratner. She was much nicer than her name sounded.

I was four years old on the day my mother dropped me off at the nursery school door. I was dressed like a doll in my cute little anklet socks with lace trim, white taffeta dress with red piping, and a small hat that resembled a flying saucer. I thought I was adorable back then, but as I glance at pictures of myself wearing this outfit, I am appalled that I went to school this way.

My mother knocked on the red door, which had since been painted blue. Mrs. Ratner came out to the landing, with a huge smile on her face. I sized her up, head to toe, admiring her glowing skin and platinum hair swept into the style of the day, a French knot. She was wearing a fashionable off-white shirtwaist-style dress that came just below her knees with low-heeled pumps to match. For a moment, I thought she looked just like my mother.

My mother always had been a stay-at-home mom. I didn't understand why I was suddenly being pawned off on strangers. Aunt Claire and Nanny were busy working at the store, but my mom could have gone in whenever she wanted.

Mrs. Ratner continued to encourage me to come inside, but I wouldn't budge. I started screaming and yelling, and the tears were falling like a heavy rain. My voice became raspy and sharp. I was turning beet red from the tantrum. I threw my hat down on the ground, snapping the elastic.

"Mommy, Mommy, why are you leaving me?" I screamed as my mother planted a kiss on my cheek and turned away, walking down the steps toward the street.

"I'll be back soon, honey," she said without turning around. "You're going to have fun. Don't worry."

Finally, still screaming, Mrs. Ratner cradled me to her waist and pulled me inside, shutting the door behind her. I felt the pang of abandonment.

Once I was inside, I heard the sounds of the other children. They were playing and smiling and laughing. I started to relax a bit, but I still had my doubts that I could like this place.

Hours later, I was given a peace offering of Jell-O chocolate instant pudding, my absolute favorite, in a small paper Dixie cup with a dollop of whipped cream on top. I took the pudding treat from Mrs. Ratner and a smile graced my face. I had a second helping and I was in my glory. Another hour went by and a few students spoke to me, but I felt they stared at me strangely. The odd girl. The one with the orthopedic shoes. The one who made a fuss. The one whose mother was much older than the other moms.

Exhausted from emotional outbursts, I fell asleep on my green cot surrounded by twenty other four-year-olds, who were spending their first day away from their mothers. Even though I relaxed a bit, I harbored a deep resentment that day against Mom. I know now why she brought me there. She had every good intention. But I felt that I was left in the hands of a stranger, and I couldn't understand why.

Looking back, I'm not sure if adopted children have a harder time separating from their parents for school or camp, but there was definitely something memorable about that day. I had a distinct feeling that I didn't fit in. I felt like I was the dog who wasn't wanted and dropped off at the animal shelter, waiting for its forever home.

The Mohair Sweater
1960

AS THE CHILD of a middle-class family I had the privilege of going on multiple vacations. This pleased me immensely even at a young age as I craved sights, sounds and activities outside my normal routine of home and the family business.

When I was about six years old, we were invited to the Catskills, which I remember my parents referring to as the "Jewish Poconos." It did not matter to me where we were going. I was on an adventure with the two people I loved most in the world. The resort may have been called Singers, since I found many vintage matchbook covers with the name embossed on it. It was a fine place and I was excited to be there. My parents had a strong zest for life at that time and their desire to enjoy all the amenities of the resort led them to make the decision to leave me alone in the hotel room which, unknowingly, would have everlasting effects on all of us.

Some short time before they left for the dance hall, I had been properly fed, bathed and tucked into bed in preparation for their leaving. The doors were locked from both inside and out. My parents felt I would be safe in the hotel room. A babysitter was never even considered.

As so often happens when we look back at childhood incidents, it is hard to grasp both what did occur and why we responded the way we did. Nonetheless, the memory of that night haunted me for decades while it tormented my mother with feelings of guilt and neglect for as long as I can remember.

Unaware of the source from which it sprang, I felt an uneasiness begin almost before the final click of the lock was in place. I imagined my parents smiling walking hand-in-hand down the corridor yet, at the same time, a rush of fear found its way to my throat and mouth. From that quivering mouth emerged a guttural, pleading primal scream.

"Please, please don't leave me. Why are you leaving? Oh, God! Don't you love me? Don't leave, don't leave me!"

Tears began and my screaming continued. Snot mixed with my salty tears ran down onto my pajama top and I leapt out of bed to race around the room, banging on the locked door and yelling at the top of my lungs, even standing on a chair to scream out the window. No one responded.

I felt terror set in, and I screamed and screamed until my voice broke down into short, raspy sobs, where no words came out. I needed something safe to hold onto. I needed my mother.

I ran to the closet and saw the stacked suitcases. I tore wildly at all the clothes and pulled out my mother's mohair sweater, the one with the light grey flowers and trim. The one she always wore to The Store on Saturdays. I had to have it, to hold it, to hold onto that piece of my mother.

After dialing "O" for operator in one last attempt to get my parents back, especially my mother, I could hear the rhythmic sound of the dance hall music pounding in the background as the operator tried to reassure me. Her young voice was soothing, but not the voice I wanted to hear. The sweater in my hands was my only link to the one person I truly needed, the person to whom I was irrevocably bonded.

Mother, the person I loved the most, the only person I wanted to belong to me, the person to whom I belonged.

Still stunned that she had left me alone in this unfamiliar hotel room, I crushed the sweater to my chest and surrendered myself to its power. It held her scent, it had been next to her skin. It was itchy, but to me it was a luxurious, mother-scented blanket. It seemed as if I couldn't get enough of it. I continued to breathe in its fragrance, a mixture of my mother's make-up and perfume, mohair fibers and all, struggling to twist and re-twist the sweater to immerse as much of myself as possible into the fabric. The thought of dying by suffocation never occurred to me, but the thought of dying of loneliness and of abandonment, would not leave my mind.

At a time, past eternity, when they finally returned, my parents found the room in great disarray and their only child in desperation lying on the bed. They saw me in a fetal position wrapped in a favorite sweater, eyes clenched tight with fear.

I heard my mother sob, "Jack, what have we done? We shouldn't have left her. She's so afraid."

Yet I still could not open my eyes.

I felt her warm presence, and when at last her arms surrounded me, I leaned into her embrace. She rocked me slowly, lovingly, but did not disturb the mohair sweater as she positioned the bed covers around me and caressed my hands. My parents had not abandoned me after all, my mother once again belonged to me, and I allowed myself to fall into a deep and peaceful sleep, wrapped safely in the mohair sweater.

My Plastic Face

AS I SAT with great anticipation, an eager second grade student awaiting the return of my wonderful teacher, Miss Stein, the small classroom held the muffled sounds of twenty-five seven year olds waiting patiently in their seats for their young, frail, and inexperienced teacher. She could have only been gone for fifteen minutes but it felt like a lifetime.

I kept looking over my shoulder at Stu, a geeky-looking boy, shorter than me, with large framed glasses and black, greasy hair staring oddly in my direction and rolling his eyes in his head. All the girls said he liked me but he was such an annoyance that there was no appreciation for little Stu.

My dearest friend, Judith, kept whispering into my ear, leaning over her seat, "He's in love with you."

The words sounded silly, and I was lost in my own fun and couldn't care less. In looking back, I occasionally wonder how his life had been since he was so unpopular in school, and due to his poor vision, he suffered impairments which forced him to be alone much of the time. Little did I realize that my own future impairments were getting ready to be launched any minute and that my face, as I knew it, was going to change in a big way.

To break the silence, students started rising from their chairs one-by-one and running to the door to see what was taking Miss Stein so long to return. We were afraid to leave the classroom, so occupying our time became the prime objective at this point. Suddenly, out of the suppressed sounds came the din, louder and louder, erupting from our voices into the classroom like a volcano getting ready to spew its fire. The sounds of chairs being scraped along the concrete floor and chalk being dragged along the blackboard did not overshadow the laughter that arose on that morning in the little second grade classroom at Shaw Avenue Elementary School in Valley Stream, New York. A free-for-all was taking place.

Judith had strong broad shoulders, blonde straight hair like a straw broom, and deep brown freckles across her nose, resembling the popular doll at the time, "Chatty Cathy." She gave me "that" look as she jumped out of her seat and grabbed my small skinny form. Up into the air I went and onto her back, legs gripping her large hips with all of my might. Before I realized what was happening I began screaming with wild abandon, "Ride-em Horsey, Ride-em Cowboy, Heehaw." I screamed louder as Judith galloped around the classroom while I was thinking I truly was Dale Evans from the once-popular television show.

Judith continued around the class, oblivious to the cacophonous sounds of the other children. The chair, made of light blonde-grained wood, stood larger than life looming two feet tall above the floor. Judith let out a yelp followed by a silence.

Bam! I hit the marble-like concrete floor of the classroom with tremendous gusto. I remember seeing the largest stars I ever saw. When I rolled over completely, dazed by what had happened, I felt blood gushing from my nose, mouth, and face, unable to speak. Through watery eyes and delirium, I saw the white shapes of my teeth embedded into the concrete floor looking like little fossils embedded into sedimentary river rock.

Instinctively, I put my hand to my face and touched the warm, flowing blood, smelling the metallic aroma and instantly vomited onto the floor time and time again.

My voice sounded like an echo coming from somewhere far away. I heard the muffled crying of the other children and the sounds of something scary and disturbing. A howling sound came out of my mouth which sounded like an animal in pain. My hand ventured to where my beautiful new and permanent front teeth had once been only to feel holes and blood in their place, and a pain that would not quit. All I can actually remember from that exact moment was fear, in its deepest form. I laid back down, unconscious to the world.

When I awoke hours later in the recovery room of a hospital, I saw the people who loved me the most looking down on me, holding my hand in theirs, with a look of confusion and devastation on their faces. I only wanted to say that I was truly sorry; sorry for changing everything, sorry that the little girl whom my mom longed for had turned ugly in a matter of seconds. That was how I felt.

Both my mom and I were going to feel pain for years to come. I, from the physical pain of the endless oral surgeries and continued life-long dental work, and, my mom from seeing her beautiful little seven-year-old girl, whom she adored, damaged in an instant.

I am not sure what hurt most that day in 1962, the physical wounds and cuts, or watching the look on my parents' faces, clearly sending the message of disappointment, for what could have been, but seeing the reality of what was.

About a month after the accident, I sat innocent and small in a courtroom, face to face with Miss Stern, the woman who created this problem. I felt anger, resentment, and rage, yet it took all I had as a young child to answer the questions put before me, which seemed like a dream.

How could I condemn this young, bright teacher who fed us snacks every day and put "good job" stickers on our papers? They say that life can change in an instant, and what changed that day was my view toward this young woman and the lack of confidence I had in myself for years to come. I eventually forgave her, and pitied her as she received disciplinary action by the school for abandoning children in a classroom.

One thing I never did, until recently, was to forgive myself, for holding this against me, against Judith, against all of those people who told me "not to smile" for the camera anymore, for the dentists who could not put my jaw and teeth back together the way they should have been, for the embarrassment from other children and young adults, and for the pain of being disfigured at an age when it mattered. As an adult, I recognized that my injury was way less important than so many other children who were injured or became sick at a young age, but the pain of non-acceptance was harder. My mom never got over this accident, nor did she accept my broken mouth as the new reality, but continued to pine for the "way I was supposed to look," the way someone regards a broken china cup with a hairline crack as no longer perfect.

My broken teeth became the center of my life for a long time following this incident and interfered with many personal and romantic relationships, well into my early twenties. I harbored this resentment for many years. It wasn't until right before my mother's death in 2008 that my insecurities vanished in an instant. I walked into her hospital room, where she was lying in bed, and she said to me, "You look beautiful, no, you are beautiful."

Those were the saving words spoken on that day which I desperately needed to hear to begin healing. Although I know and believe that I am by no means ugly, and have a universal beauty to share with the world, the scars of my childhood accident will always be more than skin deep.

The Birthday Trails

ONE OF THE most magnificent events of my life was the "birth-day trails," as my mom and I referred to them. This became a family tradition, and I always felt I was the most special child on the block, as I thought no other little girl in the entire world experienced these events, and even if they did, no mom worked harder at getting this together.

I must have been around six or seven-years old when I awoke one morning, anticipating my birthday on July 5, a hot and sticky New York summer day, anxious and excited to see my presents. When I leaped out of the daybed, plopping my feet onto the hardwood floor beneath me, something odd and shiny met my bare feet.

Lo and behold, when I looked down, there was a series of pennies, quarters, nickels, and dimes all deliberately placed in a path resembling little stepping stones, which I found led through the entire house and finally into the living room. At the culmination of this fanciful trail, filled with money, hearts, cards, and little sayings was the large array of beautifully wrapped presents of all shapes and sizes. In our living room, we had a rather ornate table, with an even more ornate lamp sitting atop it. I never liked either one, but it was a very purposeful arrangement, as it was used to hold presents for every holiday and the illumination from that lamp lent itself to a sparkling beacon of joy.

As I quietly back-tracked to my bedroom, I steadied myself to touch each coin with my pointed toe, and stooped down to read each and every note, which were lovingly placed on the floor below. All birthdays were celebrated with real meaning in the Wolf household, and mine was turning out to be even more of a gala event with this new tradition.

After the first hour went by, and my parents pretended to be asleep in their bed, I broke down and cried. As I thought about each one of those coins and words from my mom's favorite poems, some of which she wrote herself, I felt overwhelmed by the love that went into putting this little trail together. Each paper was cut into the shape of a heart or birthday cake and quoted words from Louisa May Alcott's books, "Little Women" or "Jo's Boys," two of her favorite stories. Occasionally, I would notice a scent wafting up from the tiny papers, and realized that she had sprayed her perfume onto the paper, something that we used to do many times together to make our own sachets.

My mom worked hard at the family store each day, and time was always an issue, yet she took this time for me. When I think that after a long but fun day at the annual family picnic at our home on the Fourth of July, she sat and waited until I went to bed early that evening so she could make this all materialize. It truly was a labor of love. Yet, she never drew attention to herself or complained one bit.

For each birthday or holiday, such as Christmas or Valentine's Day that followed year after year until I was eighteen years old and graduated high school, the unique trails made themselves known.

As I reflect today, on my 53rd birthday, having to celebrate without her, I want to thank my mom in particular, for taking the time to make a little girl happy, *her* little girl. To my mom, my birthday was more than just a day for parties, picnics, and presents, it was a day to remind *her* as well that she did something life-changing a long time ago, and, knowing that now, my birthday holds a much deeper meaning for me. In celebrating my birthday with the little trails, it was as if she was staking claim to my life. The poems she wrote were her deepest dreams. In fact, just a few months ago, I found a list among her private papers. Out of a notebook for her adult college classes, fell a little piece of paper. On that paper, was a list of all of the things in her life for which she was most grateful. There it was, in black and white, at the top of the list: "The birth of my daughter." It did not say "adopted" or make any reference to the fact that I wasn't her biological daughter. She said what she meant. *My* daughter.

She held that claim up high through all the years we had together. If I were to make a thank-you list today for all of the blessings she gave me, it would most certainly include the birthday trails. But the biggest thank you would be for the extreme love she had for me and how it bonded us despite many estrangements. *I am hers, and she is mine, and that is forever.*

Lost Memories

WHEN THE NIGHTMARES began, I was only six or seven years old. . I had no idea what prompted them, but in my night terrors, fires were blazing all around me. Most nights I was scared to put my face to the pillow, even with a four foot "Patti Play Pal" doll by my side to keep me company.

I felt the heat of the flames and saw them consuming me from the inside out. I would call out to my parents, who were just down the hall reading in bed. I yelled for them multiple times, and when they finally came, they would find me lying in the bed, dazed and confused, drenched in sweat.

Neither my mom nor dad realized what had happened or what to do. There was nothing they could do to make the nightmares disappear. The fire was all around me. My mom made many attempts to change the physical arrangements of the room. She moved my bed so I could see the doorway thinking it might help, but things remained the same.

I continued to dream about fire night after night, every so often seeing the face of Miss Dikeman, my first-grade teacher. I didn't like her very much. She always told us weird stories about fire or something scary.

As a young child, all I wanted was love, a mother's love. I would often look in the mirror and see a little girl who looked happy on the outside, with my lopsided, toothy grin. But inside, I felt that I was looking in on my life from the outside. I never felt a part of it.

I felt abandoned, as I struggled from day to day with a clouded identity and never let myself focus on my life.

Why was I unable to hold onto anything for very long? Why was I so frightened all the time, of every sound or facial expression or word that came out of people's mouths? What was I searching for?

As my parents made the dutiful attempt to calm me down during these nightmares, I had no voice. It felt as if the heat of the room was bearing down upon my head, my eyes, and my soul. I remember the smell; putrid and hot, and everything ugly in the world. I smelled it year after year, I can smell it now.

I faced so much abandonment in those early years that I am not sure how I survived it all. I admit that I was not the most compliant child; yet, as I take an honest look at myself, I never had an ounce of meanness in my body.

My father frightened me beyond comprehension, and his repeated scolding left permanent scars on every part of my being. I tried to block out most of my negative encounters with him, but fear had a firm hold on my heart. I knew when my father saw life his way, and when he became frustrated at the smallest thing I might have done, he pulled me by my hair and stood me up facing the wall of my room.

"Nose to the grindstone," he hollered in his usual stern voice. I smelled the lilac paint as my little nose was pressed hard against the wall. My hair tingled on my scalp as he continued to hold onto my ponytail.

"Daddy, Daddy, please stop," I pleaded. "I'm sorry, Mommy, I'm sorry," I cried through violent gasps. Nothing changed.

The veins bulged in his neck, his breath hot on my neck. The belt and the buckle made contact with my skin as I felt the pain of the metal tip and his loss of control. I felt the loss of me.

The hurt that went beyond skin deep was when I watched my mother. She stood silent in the doorway. I screamed out to her to help me in my depleted voice and cried until I had no more tears left.

I never understood what I did to warrant such a reaction from my father, and I never did understand why my mom was so afraid that she couldn't tell my father to stop. My feelings about this plagued me for many years. It is difficult to identify the feelings that you hold as a child, and to make sense of it all. But, at the same time, I did remember feeling that I was unwanted by both of my parents. This feeling was fostered by their behaviors, and I hated my mother for acting the role of an accomplice to my father's behavior. I never got the opportunity to speak with her about this in later years. I'm disappointed in myself that I didn't make this happen for me.

For most of my young childhood years, I lived in fear of what I said or how I said it, because I knew it would turn into physical torture. I never got used to the cycle of being hit and then crawling into bed with my parents to be coddled and forgiven the next day, or even hours later. It was difficult, to say the least, to have endured the fierce yelling and lengthy arguments that ensued between my parents after my punishments.

I watched my mother become someone she didn't intend to be.

The early evenings she spent in solitude, and I often heard her soft sobbing on the porch steps. I felt her sadness, but as a little girl, I didn't have any answers. Hope seemed to be waning all around us.

When I glanced at my childhood pictures, I wondered how anyone could inflict physical harm on a little child.

Why did I have to sit on the basement steps for hours in the dark with the door locked behind me, contemplating my fate?

Damn you, who did this? I thought.

I became permanently afraid of the dark. I had a feeling of detachment and aloneness. Even during the day, this darkness changed how I perceived things. I was often lost in the horror of the memories and the visions that never seemed to leave me. This provoked so many insecurities in my adult relationships, that the fear of abandonment is always with me.

The Store

FROM THE AGE of three until I graduated from high school in 1973, my life, as was my mother's, centered on the family business, Bressler's Hardware, commonly referred to as "The Store."

The way the store came into being is somewhat mysterious. My maternal grandparents, Paul and Eva Ruth Bressler, were married in New York City in 1911. Grandfather Paul was a Romanian immigrant who came through Ellis Island in the late nineteenth century along with his family. Neither of the couple's families were wealthy, but they had quite an elegant wedding ceremony and reception at the Willoughby Mansion in New York City, as I learned from the beautiful wedding program that I discovered several years ago. Beyond that, very little was known of their early married life with the exception of the birth of their two girls, Harriet Sybil and Claire Cecelia, born before 1917.

In the early 1930s, my grandfather had an unknown benefactor who provided him with funds to start a business. Who the benefactor was, and what kind of business my grandfather initially started, remains unknown. My mother was always tight-lipped about the subject. However, plans were made to buy a hardware store in the mid-1930s and the grand opening was held soon thereafter.

My grandfather suffered a tragic mental breakdown not long after the store opened, only to die days later in a mental institution. My mother, at nine years of age, bore witness to this terrifying event and acknowledged in later years that her father was carried out of the house in a straightjacket yelling and screaming something unintelligible.

As she recalled the tale in a conversation we had several years before she died, I asked her about her father. She began to cry violently and threw her hands around her face saying, "Oh, my God, no, no, I don't want to remember. Nanette, don't make me remember."

I was so disturbed by her outburst that I made a point never to question her again on the subject. I realized how the death of her dad significantly changed her life forever, as it was revealed to me in a short story she wrote in junior high school entitled "I Grow Up."

"I have tasted joy and not so long ago, although it seems like centuries, I experienced a sorrow, the memory of which can never be erased from my mind. I lost my childhood playmate and fairytale hero, through the death of my Dad," she wrote.

Grandfather Paul's mother blamed Eva Ruth, insisting that it was her constant nagging that led to his breakdown and demise. Ties between the two sides of the family were completely severed after his death and no one dared mention it again.

So, it was Eva Ruth, along with her two daughters, who established Bressler's Hardware in 1936. The store was located on Linden Boulevard in the business section of Queens County at a time when life was simpler and trolleys coexisted with automobiles. The beautiful large brick building where the store was housed included two five-room apartments above it. There was a sprawling dark basement, which became a playground for me, harboring rooms full of exciting and mysterious old toys. Some of these toys dated back to the mid-1800s, like the Ginny dolls with long eyelashes that felt like real hair and deep blue eyes that opened and closed. The old Mickey Mouse "Steamboat Willie" cup and saucer tea set was one of my favorites. It is now displayed in my writing room in my home.

The business flourished over the years under the strong-willed guidance of my grandmother and the help of her two daughters. My mother was the bookkeeper while my beloved Aunt Claire designed award-winning window displays and handled merchandising. There were other employees as well, but it always remained a family operation, largely run by women.

Living above the store was convenient, and the profitable business allowed my mother and aunt to attend schools of their choosing as young adults. When my mother and father married in 1950 and made a home in the suburbs of Long Island, Grandma Eva and Aunt Claire continued to live in the upstairs apartment until the summer of 1973. After my parents married, my mother continued to work at the store. My father became a well-known fixture of the business, particularly on weekends.

I remember feeling loved and cherished at the store, because it allowed my mother and I to spend time together, as well as giving me a small glimpse into her childhood. I spent many hours in the upstairs apartments, and, of course, there was the basement, which held high adventure for a little girl.

After school was out, my mother and I would get a snack and head to the store. I remember setting up a space for myself, located near a small counter, where I could perch myself atop an old wooden stool that creaked from age, smelling the sawdust gathered on the floor and taking in the customer transactions, all the while doing homework. I also recall dashing up the steep hidden steps to the apartment above to get a piece of my grandma's homemade blueberry pie or to take a nap on the old saggy, yet comfy, bed in her room. I loved to cuddle on the knobby white bedspread, feeling the little pom-poms on the spread. One of the most interesting features in the apartment was the gigantic skylight in the tiny bathroom. If I strained hard enough, I could stand on the ledge of the claw foot tub and look up through the roof and see the sun shining in, casting giant shadows on the skylight. I pretended that it led to the stars.

The neighborhood surrounding the store was lively in the early 1960's, and every store held a different kind of story. The dry-cleaning business directly adjacent to the west side of the store, La Parisien, was owned by Vi, an Italian immigrant widow who spoke little English. Several doors down the street, there was a meat market owned by a large red-haired man with a red moustache. He was the town grocer and always had a small treat when we stopped in for our weekly fare. Across the street there was an "everything" sort of store with a soda fountain and pharmacy. It was owned by Theresa, a mulatto woman, who had purchased it from the previous owners. I remember drinking hundreds of egg cream sodas there during my childhood. The famous chocolate egg cream does not seem to exist anywhere but in New York. It consists of club soda, fresh milk, real eggs, and good old-fashioned chocolate syrup. When it is prepared correctly you can slurp the meringue foam on top, acquiring a foamy moustache which tickled my upper lip while relishing in the chocolaty goodness.

When Theresa tired of that business, she opened a record shop further down the street on Linden Boulevard and appropriately named it Theresa's Record Hut. On one particular day, upon entering the store, I was greeted by her little Snoopy look-alike dog, Penny, who soon after, became my first dog, my very own "Penny Poo." Sadly, Penny was hit by a car in the neighborhood about two years later and subsequently had to be put to sleep.

When I was approaching eight years old, during the height of the civil rights movement, I was excited to be going to Radio City Music Hall for the first time. My heart was pounding and I had butterflies in my stomach as I recall boarding the city bus in front of the store with my mother. I looked at the driver, then around the bus at the other passengers. Suddenly I blurted out, "Mommy, look at all the chocolate people!"

My mother shoved me quickly into the corner of the seat, and with an air of extreme embarrassment, said to me, "Be quiet, we will discuss it later." Of course, I was terribly confused, having formed no concept of race whatsoever and not understanding why she was so upset.

At a time when I was growing up and beginning to be exposed to the world around me, the issue of race was handled less than ideally by my family and created a significant estrangement between my mom, dad, and me for years to come. I was never told anything particularly negative about Negroes, as African-Americans were called at the time, but the message was conveyed that there was a marked difference between hiring or working with them and being friends with them or, God-forbid, intermarrying.

Grandma Eva hired Mr. Dobson, who was about seventy years old, and the blackest man I had ever seen. Mr. Dobson was one of the nicest people that I had known in my young life and amused me with his funny and tall tales about his family. We often laughed and ate to-gether in the store. He treated me kindly as if I were his own granddaughter, and often brought in special pastries that his wife made fresh that morning. I was intrigued by his choice of clothes, almost formal for a hardware store, and one day I asked him, "Mr. Dobson, why do you wear those straps to hold up your socks and sleeves?"

He replied in his exaggerated Southern drawl, "These straps, hmm, they holds up the clothes. Theys are called garters. Hmmm, yes, Missus, they are all the clothes I has, except for the ones I wear to church."

I thought he looked sharp and I was sure glad he worked for my grandmother. Dottie, another employee, a middle-aged white woman, was included in family events and the upstairs luncheons. Looking back, I felt bad for Mr. Dobson, as he was not included in these events. My family was not color blind.

As I continued to grow in body and mind and discovered my in-dependence, I began to see the world through my own eyes and formed my own strong opinions. Once begun, the process of inde-pendent thought moved like a rolling stone gaining a momentum. In time, this would lead to disharmony between my mother and me, fueled by my father's iron hand.

By the time I was nine years old, I gained knowledge of new things, and learned a bit about running a business. Many of the cus-tomers asked for me by name, and I became Grandma Eva's little helper, earning a small allowance in the process. I learned how to iden-tify paint colors from the Benjamin Moore paint chart and actually knew the difference between their brands, particularly Sani-flat and High-Gloss, as well as the difference between floor paint and porch paint. I was a little entrepreneur and as time went by, my responsibili-ties increased. Working the cash register was something I learned quickly, even though my math skills at school were taking a nosedive.

I thought making change was infinitely more practical than "new math."

Interacting with the customers, getting to know their backgrounds, made me feel like they were my own clients. When visitors entered the store on a warm summer day, they would be greeted with the smell of sawdust on the floor or of an oilcloth hanging on racks. Grandma Eva would be sitting by the door in her orange woven beach chair. They would nod to her and ask, "How's little Nanette today? I need her to mix me up a quart of Hibiscus Pink." Aunt Claire had taught me so much and it made her proud to see me working with the paints. She often complimented me on my eye for color, which is something my husband boasts about when I decorate our home.

Years went by, and in the summer of 1968 when I was thirteen years old, the store where I had always felt safe and secure, was robbed. A few local hoodlums appeared in the middle of a Saturday afternoon, our busiest time. In addition to the customers, my parents, Grandma Eva, Aunt Claire, Mr. Dobson, Dottie, and I were all present, going about our usual tasks. At first, no one was sure what was going on. We heard raised voices as Peter, the ringleader, and his crew skulked through the aisles. Then Peter tried to bully my grandmother into opening the cash register, something he had attempted on three previous occasions. She simply refused, planting her feet solidly on the wooden floor, head held high, shoulders pushed back, and boldly stated, "Peter, take this candy on the counter, go ahead now. You don't belong here." With her throaty voice conveying impatience and irritation, she continued, "Go on, and get out of here now. I'll be calling your mother as soon as I get a chance."

Then, the unthinkable happened. Peter and his cohorts pulled out guns. At that point, some of the customers fled through the open front door. Not knowing if the guns were even loaded, we were terrified. Nine of us, including three customers, who couldn't leave, were forced at gunpoint into the small bathroom at the rear of the store. With all of us crammed together, smelling each other's nervous sweat, I pressed against my mother, my fear reaching panic level as my heart pounded and I shook uncontrollably. I thought to myself, will my mom protect me?

We heard the clang of the cash register being forced opened, and the sound of breaking glass and immediately after, footsteps running on the hardwood floor, as the thugs headed for the door. My dad, who heard all of this commotion, bolted up the basement steps in hot pursuit after them, his own police special in hand. He chased them down Linden Boulevard. Not thinking clearly, the rest of us ran out of the bathroom and followed closely behind. The stolen money and other valuables were stashed somewhere along the way as some of the thieves continued their escape throughout the neighborhood.

Bang! Peter fired a shot behind him and hit my father in the calf. I heard his scream and saw him fall to the concrete. He was sixty-one years old, lying in the middle of the street. I can still smell the sweat emanating from all of us, and see and feel the burning tears of terror and despair. Luckily for us all, Peter ended up in the pokey and my father had stitches. Nonetheless, it was traumatic for everyone.

For so many years, the store had meant stability, a place where I was surrounded by family and long-time customers who had become our friends. Life was good then, very good, even though political turmoil filled the air. The store was busy and provided a good living for all of us, not to mention the increase in my weekly allowance. There was money to spare. But the best thing was that we were all close as a family, and I thanked God for that feeling every day.

As time went on and I approached my sophomore year in high school, things began to change. I was no longer satisfied to be part of the simple existence that the family business provided. Whatever it was that once intrigued me about the sights and smells of Benjamin Moore paints, the green Corning Ware, or the once famous Ginny dolls, was gone. I still accompanied my parents to the store on Saturdays and after school several days a week, but I was starting to harbor a poor attitude, and it was evident that I wasn't the only one who was changing.

Week after week, I studied my mother and father and saw that they were rapidly aging. My father was already sixty-six years old and slowing down. Robberies in the neighborhood had become a frequent occurrence, and the store closed earlier each month. Trying to compete with the big discount stores like Great Eastern Mills was next to impossible, and many days we didn't make a sale until mid-afternoon. I observed my grandmother's face and saw extreme sadness in her eyes. The store was dying a slow death, my parents were aging, and I was leaving a huge part of my childhood behind. Without the anchor of a bustling business, the family seemed to be drifting apart and tensions were high amongst all of us with the unknown right around the corner.

Eventually, things became unbearable and a decision to sell was made for us. We all mourned the loss of my grandmother who died in May of 1978, but it was my mom who was left the most devastated. She had lost her future, her past, and her present in her dying mother. My mom was left without a focal point in her life and my dad was fully retired. Once I graduated college that June, I married my first husband, Tom. The store was sold off in 1979 to a Baptist church, changing all of our lives forever. It left me feeling confused and alone, without any real connections to a family in which I already felt adrift. The summer of 1978 marked the end of an era and the store faded into memory.

Intermediate Years

AS I GREW older, life became more complicated and always shrouded by a marked tension in the family. I was still trying harder than ever to get my mom's attention away from my dad, and I felt that she was pushing me aside. Childhood life became difficult for me to handle, and sent me into a whirlwind.

I was getting ready to graduate from sixth grade at Shaw Avenue Elementary School. I felt alone and isolated. I did not feel like I had any real or caring friends. I felt like I didn't belong to anyone or anything. In fact, at some points in elementary school, I had no friends. My teeth were still deformed, which caused me extreme anxiety. I had the fear of going to junior high school looking very much like an ugly eleven-year-old.

Mom suggested that we go on a shopping spree one afternoon and have lunch together. When she wasn't working in the store, she was busy at home being a full-time mom. I felt special when she asked me, and relished in the invitation as I looked forward to the event. As the week went on, she never mentioned it again, and it surprised me on the day that we planned to go she announced we were not spending the day together because she had to work in the school auditorium and set the stage for the upcoming graduation.

Mom was the current president of the PTA for the school and was very much involved. This made me feel proud, but at the same time I felt jealous and neglected, that all of her extra time was spent with other people and she was ignoring me. I never knew how to talk with her and let her know my true feelings, so it became another opportunity to stuff my feelings and react later.

So, off we went back to the auditorium after school to meet the other moms. Mom continued to mill about the room, chatting happily with the mothers and some of their children who attended the school. I began to feel more and more isolated, as she never once spoke to me while we were there. I tried to ask her questions, but she politely shooed me away with short answers.

After several hours of being ignored, and not knowing why, a rage built up deep inside of me along with hurt packed in between.

I ran down the hallway from the auditorium and bolted out of the school door. I continued to run away onto the main streets of the town for what seemed like several miles. I was exhausted from crying and running. I made my way along the railroad tracks near a popular stretch of road, called Merrick Road. I managed to hide under an overpass structure as I continued to cry and heave.

It was fast approaching sunset, and with no sign of anyone coming to find me, I felt that I wasn't important enough to be found. I knew deep inside that I had created a firestorm. Although it seemed purposeful at the time, the outcome was not what I had expected.

The police arrived with my parents in tow. I do not recall how they found me, but I saw the look on my mother's face. It was one of hurt, pain, and desperation over something neither one of us understood.

After the police drove away, my father grabbed my shoulders and shook me as he screamed and yelled into my ear, "What the hell is wrong with you, you crazy kid? Do you realize how much trouble you are in?" he ranted.

My mom bombarded me with questions about why I behaved as I did. She sobbed softly.

To this very day, I cannot say why I caused such pain for them, other than I was hurting so bad. I didn't know what else to do. This event was never spoken of again in our family. Mom never consoled me or reassured me after the incident. She just wanted to forget it and pretend that it never happened. I felt like she wanted to pretend that I never happened.

If I could talk about this with Mom today, I would apologize to her for this childhood event, and unveil the truth about how upset and neglected I felt. I would have asked her why she gave up her promise to be with me.

I cried into my pillow that evening, as I heard my parents' muffled voices through the bedroom wall. My biggest fear was that they would give me away because of how I chose to act. I didn't want to be sent to the Salvation Army's Home for Wayward Girls. All of the bad girls were sent there. I certainly had lost credibility as a good and loving daughter. I heard the word "damaged" emerge from the next room and contemplated leaving again.

Because of this incident, and similar ones over the years, it has taken me a long time to dismiss a broken promise. I suppose that most people could have gotten over this, but I never did. Even though I had no clue that I was adopted at this point, this incident made me feel that I wasn't part of any family.

When I think back into my early childhood and pre-teen years, I knew that my mother felt my pain. She endured a very strict and un-loving mother and the agonizing loss of her dad. We were alike in so many ways, yet I fought hard not to "be her."

Mom and I continued to struggle as a mother and daughter in different ways. Once we made it through elementary school, and the first "running away" incident was behind us, I felt excited to be a teen-ager.

We occasionally did the usual things that a mother and daughter would do, but I always felt that it was an act. It felt as if it was part of a play, that needed to be scrutinized and constantly revised. It was as if I was an outsider, looking into our family without having a real part. I was neither aggressive nor combative at this point, just a wee bit different.

Mom and I went to buy my first bra at Abraham and Straus. This whole activity evolved after a close friend joked about how skinny I was. "You're so flat," Sue said.

I was embarrassed by my gawky frame, and perfectly straight up and down appearance, and I couldn't imagine what a bra would look like on me. All I wanted were the straps to show under my tank tops and the back clasp to stick out. I wanted to wear the bra as a badge of honor, to show I was a normal girl.

There really wasn't any honor involved, come to think of it, but it was a sure way to fit in by the start of junior high school. I remember looking at my mom's face when I insisted that she leave the dressing room. She looked hurt. She handed me piles of bras over the top of the dressing room curtain because I wouldn't allow her to see me naked. When I think back about how many times in my infant years and early childhood that my mother cleaned my wounds, or wiped my behind for having an unexpected bowel movement, or cleaned up vomit from a night of the stomach flu, it was ridiculous that I was so shy in front of her. I knew she yearned to be more accepted by me.

Yet, we were alike in this respect, as I never really saw her out of her clothes at all, except for the occasional trying on of outfits at home, when she was getting ready to go out with my dad on a Friday or Saturday night. This ritual was an intimate time of mother and daughter connection that I cherished. I sat on the bed, feet dangling, resting my chin in my hands, airing my opinions about her clothes and her weight. I can remember every mole on her arms and back, and recall her everyday scent, a combination of Mennen's medicated powder, body lotion, hair spray, and sweat all mixed into one.

As I helped her zip up the dresses or clasp the back of her skirts, I relished in her need for me at a time when I felt so lonely, both in and out of the house.

Occasionally, we would have short conversations about her outfits. If I tried to grab her bras or sweaters and put them on my skinny frame, she would laugh out loud and say, "Nanette, stop being so silly." That was a phrase that she used often to denote lightheartedness or, when she was truly frustrated or perturbed. Either way, I didn't mind it, as she showed me that she was paying attention to what I had said and that felt good.

When I turned twelve in the summer of 1967, Mom, Dad, and I took a summer vacation to kick off my junior high career. We drove from Long Island, New York, in one day to Provincetown, Cape Cod in Massachusetts for my first time visiting this popular vacation spot.

Back in the late sixties, Provincetown was quite pristine and did not have half of the people on the island as there is today. Most of the townspeople were artists of every variety, business owners and eccentric types. We drove on the back roads along US 1, taking in the scenery and salt air. I was looking forward to the weeklong trip.

We all shared one room, but I was uncomfortable being in the same room with both of my parents together. I felt that I was invading my parents' privacy. I never thought of either one of them as being affectionate toward each, other than the occasional quick kiss on the lips for good morning or good night.

I wanted to spend as much time as I could outdoors, and seeing all of the Cape Cod sights. Mom and I climbed the tall and majestic dunes hand in hand. We both laughed as we almost rolled down the side and into the sea foam below. Mom and I took the time to wander the street fairs, while my dad stayed close to the hotel.

Soon after, we were flagged down by an artist who drew beautiful chalk portraits. Mom insisted I get one. Since I still had the remnants of my damaged teeth, and had not received any relief from that injury since second grade, I was worried that the artist would ask me to smile. But he didn't, and I sat for the portrait. The artist did an exquisite job with the drawing. He drew lines with the pastels, and emphasized parts of my face and hair that I never knew existed. The artist took my mouth and turned it into something beautiful. He lessened my anxiety with each stroke of the chalk, as if he knew my pain.

I don't remember his name, but I am thankful for one picture that I proudly hung on the wall.

My dad mounted the painting in the hallway at my childhood home, and then later displayed it on their condo wall when they moved to Florida in 1980. He pointed to it whenever a newcomer came to the house. It was one of the few pictures that were displayed during my adolescent and adult years in my parents' home.

To this day, my husband refuses to let me change anything about it, including the massive gilded frame that my father bought when we returned home from Provincetown. Robin said, "It looks perfect just the way it is."

Many embarrassing moments followed in the next few years and life was a roller coaster ride. One of these that stood out as I recall it, was, as I entered my eighth-grade year in junior high school. I was close to fourteen years of age, and I was still conscious about my under developing body, bra and all.

I had to recite a very important speech in my eighth-grade English class. I felt uncomfortable speaking in front of a group, so I groomed myself for weeks and prepared as much as I could. I stood tall in front of my thirty classmates. My palms dripped sweat and my hands shook. I locked my knees together to keep me from falling over.

Several minutes into the speech, the students started to stir. I heard their whispered comments. As I looked down at my index cards in my hands, I caught a glimpse of a white fluffy tissue. It seemed to move in slow motion as it fell to the floor. I looked down with horror as several more fell. The tissues were moving upwards out from my bra and onto the front of my shirt. I stuffed the tissues into my bra earlier that morning to make up for the lack of development. I felt the tears well up in my eyes and a lump forming in my throat. I stood there, completely still. I could not utter a sound. The heat of my face from embarrassment could have boiled water. I dropped the note cards on the floor and ran from the room and did not look back. I heard raucous laughter coming from my classroom.

I barely survived that incident only to have another embarrassing moment several weeks later. I was cursed with my period for the first time. It wouldn't have been so bad, but I was a late bloomer, and my friends never let me forget it. Neither did my parents.

I came home from school one day and watched as my mother looked on with disbelief and shock when my father showed up after work with a cake that read, "You are a woman now."

Even though Mom was as horrified as I, she was not brave enough to let my father know how badly he embarrassed and ridiculed me. He sang, as I cowered. After that moment, I vowed to keep my personal life secret from both of them for a long time.

Estrangement

HIGH SCHOOL WAS one of the most challenging times in my life. Of course, that is true for most people at that age. However, my challenge was different. I didn't know who I belonged to, yet I lived with my family for at least sixteen years.

I spent as much time as I could alone in my room each day. I read every book in the house and the daily newspapers. I grappled with the meaning of my life. I soon found an answer to my problems.

Little red pills.

I found them in my grandma's medicine cabinet. They were crammed into a leaded glass jar with a decorative top. There must have been at least sixty pills. I wasn't sure what they were until after I swallowed the first pill. I think they were phenobarbital or Quaaludes or some odd name that I learned about in Health class that year. I wasn't sure what they were doing in my grandma's medicine cabinet. Maybe she was taking them for arthritis pain. I didn't care what they were because I was looking for relief from my day to day feeling of sadness and non-belonging.

The pill went down without a hitch. I felt sleepy. I laid down on Grandma's bed, and fell fast asleep wrapped in the softness of the bed linen.

Two hours later, my mom shook me, saying, "Nanette, Nanette, what's wrong? Wake up, wake up. It's almost five o'clock. Time to go home."

I barely heard her words. It seemed like I was in a tunnel and I couldn't move. Finally, I stirred and sat up, leaning against the head-board. I felt dazed and confused, but at the same time, blissfully de-tached. Detached from my problems, from my family, detached from me. It was a good feeling. I wanted more of it. As I slowly made my way to the bathroom, woozy and wobbly, I thought to myself, did the pills do this? Whoa.

I caught my reflection in the tiny bathroom mirror. I steadied my-self on the antique subway tile. I smiled into the mirror. I looked the same on the outside, but boy oh boy, did I feel good on the inside. I guess weighing only 100 pounds soaking wet caused the pills to have an exaggerated effect. Just when I was feeling like I was floating, I heard Mom's voice.

"Nanette, Nannnnnette," my mom called again loudly from the kitchen. "We need to go home now! Your father will be home soon and I have to fix dinner. Get your stuff and let's get going."

I obliged her and we were on our way.

I could barely hold my head up during the short twenty-minute ride home. When we got into the house, I ran inside and dropped off my school bag, and hung my coat in the downstairs closet. I didn't know how I was going to get through dinner. I was afraid of questions. I needed more pills.

Several hours went by. The dinner dishes were tucked safely back into the cupboard, and I got ready for bed. I kissed my mom and dad goodnight and fell into bed.

The next thing I knew it was the following morning, and my Timex Baby Ben alarm was ringing in my ear, signaling the start of a school day.

Another day. Two more pills.

I gathered my school bag together, and jammed a second set of clothes into a small cloth bag. I left wearing tights, a mid-length jean skirt, boots, and a modest turtleneck that fit on my skinny frame without showing any possibility of cleavage or breast movement. My mother would approve. My father never saw me as he had already left for work.

School hours in New York were nine until three regardless of the grade level. My mother continued to make my lunch, even though I could have done it myself. There was something very special about her lunches. They were simple in substance: salami or turkey sandwich on pumpernickel or rye bread, mustard, juice, fruit, and a carrot stick. But, the part I liked best were the little notes that she placed in the wax paper for my eyes only.

The notes were often quotes from some of her favorite books or plays, such as *Little Women* or Shakespeare. The quotes were her way of staying in touch with me at a time that we were on the verge of disappearing as a mother and daughter.

Her favorite was a few lines from "In the Garret" from *Little Women*. She could recite them by heart:

"Four little chests all in a row,
Dim with dust, and worn with time,
All fashioned and filled, long ago,
By children now in their prime.
Four little keys hung side by side,
With faded ribbons, brave and gay,
When fastened there, with childish pride
Long ago, on a rainy day."

The harder she tried to be part of my life, the more I felt that she was prying and didn't deserve to know more of what was inside of my heart and head. Again, as I look back at my earlier life, I feel that more of my personality was shaped by my secret adoption, wanting the closeness, but never knowing how to accept that closeness when it came around.

I headed off to school knowing that this day was going to be different. Armed with a full bottle of red pills in my bag and my defiant scanty clothes to change into, I felt confident that any insults that came from stray students in the hallway would be well defended.

My favorite class was French. I loved how Mr. Hunt, who taught all languages in the school, sat perched atop his worn out wooden oak chair and turned a pencil in his ear while letting the "language of love" flow. Everyone thought it was disgusting, but it intrigued me for some reason. He had a distinct look with his European peg leg suits and skinny ties, and most students loved his class.

I had a knack for French, as my mother spoke it on occasion and recited poems from famous French poets. She always walked around saying, "Oui, Oui, Nanette!"

After this class, school usually took a nosedive. I did not enjoy the remaining flavor of the day with less challenging electives. I asked for a hall pass and disappeared into the grey and beige metal bathroom stalls and, with my bottle of juice, I struggled to choke down two red pills. I was never good with swallowing tablets or pills. Most of the time they got spit back into the sink or glass.

It didn't take long for the full effect to begin. I wobbled and bounced along the hard, green corridor walls, trying to find my way back to class. Without talking to anyone, I managed to slide into my wooden seat in Mr. Rosen's Bookkeeping 101 class. He gave me a quick glance, but not enough to draw attention from others.

All of a sudden, I felt a drowsiness overcome me. I kept leaning my head down closer and closer to the desk, fighting off the effect of the red pills. I wanted to be alone and savor the moment in my brain where no one called me "Bucktooth Annie," made fun of my freckles or flat chest, or teased me for having older parents.

I wanted to be free of the demands of friends who were not really acting as true friends, but always expecting something in return for their friendship. I wanted to be free of my growing sexuality that rose up at the most inconvenient moments, when I knew that I would end up being the wrong girl or the bad girl or the girl who just wanted to be held and loved, only after giving more. They called it "putting out" in those days.

I was just starting to doze off, when I noticed that Vita turned toward me and whispered, "Meet me after school today. I have something to tell ya. We'll be waiting for ya outside by the back part of the park. You betta be there."

I could barely nod, but I gave her a play.

Vita and her gang were the sleazy girls, the ones who did put out and cheated off of other people's papers, or who held you hostage for something stupid. She was part of an Italian network of kids who lived in the town. They had decent parents, but they were rebellious like the kids in the movie "Rebel Without a Cause." I feared Vita and everything she stood for, yet at the same time, she intrigued me with her toughness. I longed for acceptance.

I was still very much a good girl. Born to be successful, follow the rules, and accept the love that was given to me if it came my way. This was a time where I longed for the closeness with my mom but couldn't seem to get there. She was so busy with the store, particularly in the winter months and summers. She catered to my father's every need. She was always in a rush for something, so it seemed.

The bell startled me. It was time to leave Mr. Rosen's class, and the fear of meeting Vita set in.

Just as I was getting ready to pick up my books and bag and go, Mr. Rosen pulled me aside, and asked, "Miss Wolf, are you feeling ok? Did you get enough sleep last night?" His voice held true concern.

I wanted to tell him *I'm escaping,* Mr. Rosen, but I couldn't do it. Instead I lied, "Of course, Mr. Rosen, I just stayed up late studying for my French exam. It's hard stuff."

He seemed to be satisfied with my reply and left it at that. I hurried to my next class.

It was nearing the end of the school day, and I was starting to bite my nails with fervor. When the bell rang at three, I jumped out of my seat in Math class and stuffed some books into my locker. I raced toward the far end of the park adjacent to the school. I was still a little bit groggy, but feeling good.

I could smell the pungent odor of European cigarettes combined with wet maple leaves as I approached the park. I saw Vita and her cronies leaning on a fence.

"Come over heh," she said. "Whatcha got in that bag?"

I looked down. "A change of clothes," I said.

"What for?" she asked.

"I was going to put on something more comfortable after school." I felt like saying, *I'm gonna look like a bad girl like you,* Vita. But I kept my mouth shut.

She said, "Here, have a puff."

I made a face to show I didn't care about smoking.

Vita invited me to a party. I wasn't ready to hang out with her, but I sensed there was a motive for why she needed to see me. Most likely cheating on a test.

No sooner than the thought entered my mind, did she say loudly, "Hey, Nahnet, Berta and I were wondrin', you know, right, if you would help us with our homework in Rosen's class. Uh, ya' know, he doesn't want us to come for help anymore. But, uh, I need help with my test and so does Berta. Ain't that right, sweetness?" She turned towards Berta, a.k.a. Roberta, and gave her a wink.

"Sure, I'll help you. But you can't come to my house, because my parents won't be home until late, and they don't want people they don't know coming to the house."

"Yeah, well, that's okay, we gotcha," said Vita. "I'll see you in class tomorrow and we can figure it out then, okay?"

Before I could say another word, they lit up another smoke and walked away from me, leaving me feeling uneasy. All of this big fuss just for homework help. It didn't sound kosher to me, but I let it go.

I hurried back to the school gym, used the facilities without bothering to change my clothes, and walked home.

Aunt Mickey

AUNT MICKEY MADE a grand faux-pas the day she revealed my secret adoption. There was no doubt about it that she would hurt me or my mother by revealing such sensitive information. We were mourning my father. She didn't know the whole story and had tried to make conversation.

I loved my Aunt Marion, or Mickey as everyone called her. I considered her to be a surrogate mother for most of my life, even though she lived almost sixty miles away from me in Westchester County.

I loved her because she was true to herself. I loved her transparency. I loved the way she embraced life and lived it to the fullest. She did things to make you laugh. She put out stewed prunes in cute little dishes the night before for breakfast. She cleared your plate from the dinner table while your fork was still in your mouth. She held her cigarette in her large hand the way a man would hold it, between the thumb and forefinger. She leaned forward in her chair like she was going to say something important, but blew out a big puff of smoke instead.

She wasn't my favorite aunt, though. That position in life was reserved for my Aunt Claire, Mom's sister, but Mickey ran a close second.

Aunt Mickey gave up all of her life's dreams to take care of her Russian-born parents, Frank and Ida Wolf. She cared for them until they died in 1968. She married at sixty years old for the first time. Uncle Eddie died only nine years later because he refused to take his insulin. His death was devastating to all of us, but Aunt Mickey took it in stride, like everything else she did.

It was that special bond which existed between us. I could be free of judgement, free of a parent's glare, and free to smoke cigarettes if I wanted to. She saw things just as they were and never tried to assume anything.

We both shared a secret. I was adopted, and her real name was Mary Woolff. I discovered this after Mom died, as I was left to clean out her safe deposit box. I pulled out her old and ragged birth certificate, and was surprised to see her name wasn't Marion or Mickey. I had hoped to find my true birth certificate hiding alongside hers. Unfortunately, the box's contents revealed nothing about me.

There was no one living from my father's side of the family to ask about my adoption, except my cousin Stuart in Florida. He reacted like he had no clue and didn't care. It was just another fact to him.

Soon after my father died, Aunt Mickey and I saw each other more often. She became the elder friend on whose shoulder I could cry, or share joyous occasions. I had the perfect opportunity to sit down with her and ask her about my adoption and let her know that she had revealed a secret. I knew that she wouldn't refuse me, but the fact was, that I felt she would feel guilty that she had betrayed Mom's trust.

Obviously, she was not aware that Mom had not shared the whole story. It was a touchy situation, and I didn't want Aunt Mickey to be put in that position. Similarly, I couldn't hurt my mother's feelings by letting her know that I knew I was adopted. Aunt Mickey was one of the few people Mom could talk with, and I felt that to sever that relationship would have been unkind and irresponsible. So, I kept my mouth shut and loved her as much as I could. I let her love me too.

One of the ways that she added balance to my life was when I was a high school student. I was showing my true incorrigible side. Mom and I were estranged, yet living in the same house. Aunt Mickey invited me to spend a weekend with her in Mt. Vernon, New York, several miles from her family homestead. Aunt Mickey sensed angst within our family, and made a point to cover for me by telling my mom that she needed extra help around the house.

I jumped into my 1970 cherry edition 442 Cutlass (my dad's pride and joy) and hightailed it up north to Westchester. As I crossed the Throgs Neck Bridge, I glanced up and remembered a bad dream that I had every time I was sick as a young child. It was always the same. A rabid squirrel stood high and large on the top of the bridge, reaching down with his huge claws, foaming at the mouth, eyes red and blazing fire, ready to consume me. I never knew what caused the dream, but somehow associated it with my sad home life.

I didn't see the squirrel this time, and figured that was a good sign and kept driving. I was ecstatic that I was headed to my aunt's, where I could feel close to someone, and, at the same time, feel the impending freedom flowing like a river. This was a true getaway for mind and spirit.

I can still visualize Mickey's large one-bedroom apartment, sunny and warm and everything in its place. Aunt Mickey liked her sleep, so I was assigned the pull-out sofa in the living room, which suited me just fine as I felt like a college student who had their own space in the dorm. I had the TV all to myself.

Sometime later in the day, Mickey asked, "Hey, Nan, do you want a cig?" She broke out the Benson and Hedges Ultra-Light 100's before I could reply.

"Sure, Aunt Mickey. You know, I really don't smoke hardly at all, but I'll take one."

"You don't have to lie to me, Nanette, I know you've been smoking. Your mother said she was afraid you were and was upset about it.

As far as I'm concerned, as long as you don't make it a full-time habit, you're Ok."

Acceptance. She lit both of our cigarettes and handed one to me. I took it and puffed like a pro. We sat up almost all night, smoking, laughing, and confessing. She spoke to me about her life growing up with six brothers and sisters, of course, my dad being one of them. She spoke of how she learned to drive much later in life, and that she never liked it. When her family sold the old Victorian home, the 1942 egg-plant-colored Packard went with it. The large white steering wheel that reminded me of ivory was always there to allure me. The car was an icon. Everyone loved to sit in the worn-out leather seats. Including me. It is one of my fondest memories of the old mansion.

Aunt Mickey listened to me speak of my dad's behavior, my mom's estrangement, and how I didn't fit in. Even though there was never a mention of adoption at the time, I felt connected to her in a way that I didn't feel with mom. It wasn't that she had different rules or allowed late nights with vices, it was that her heart was open and free, and she listened with it one hundred percent. I didn't want advice. I didn't want solutions. I only wanted to belong to someone who saw me how I was.

When I left Aunt Mickey's apartment at the end of the weekend, I felt cleansed. I felt elated that she called me a great driver. I felt confident when she said I was a good shopper and let me pick out her groceries even though her cooking would rival a well-known chef.

When I drove back home on a refreshing fall Sunday afternoon, I could smell her scent lingering on my jacket when she hugged and kissed me goodbye. She still gave me a hard pinch on the cheek. She was over the top with it on occasion, but I always would feel her kindness lingering for hours afterward. Times spent with Mickey always gave me the opportunity to look at life from a positive angle. It made me think of what would have happened if she were my mother, at a time when mine wasn't good enough. It let me know the feeling of a mother's love can be all around you, even in unlikely places.

Part Two
Life Unhinged

Things I Couldn't Get Over

1. My parents did not come to my wedding when I married Robin.

I HATED WHAT happened. I held a grudge for many years. Since 1982, when Robin and I first met in St. Thomas, my mother never once asked about my social life. I called her every week as I struggled to get to the pay phone outside of the Charlotte Amalie Post Office. I stood in the enormous line for hours in the humidity and unforgiving tropical sun. I just wanted to hear her voice and know that she was still thinking of me, even though we were a thousand miles away from each other.

I had bad dreams that when I saw my mother next, she wouldn't know who I was or wouldn't accept me as her daughter.

When I met Robin, I knew that we were going to be married at some point. We came from different backgrounds in New York, but we were both people who loved life and enjoyed new experiences.

I recall the conversation we had one day on the phone. I was standing in the kitchen of the William Booth Boys Home, awaiting lunch to be prepared for the kids who resided there. "Hey, Mom, it's me. How are you guys? Is everything okay back in New York? I miss you all so much."

How's Sarah Lee?" I rattled on. "Is she still trying to sleep on your bed? Isn't she cute? She likes to be brushed in the evening before bed. Thanks so much for keeping her while I'm gone."

She briefly asked about Kathy, my friend from college, who came with me to St. Thomas, much to her father's chagrin.

"Yeah, Kathy's doing okay," I reassured her. "She loves working at the parochial school. I'm so glad I left St. Patrick's and went to work for the group home on the hill. It's so much better, and I'm making a ton of money. Tell Daddy I'm making a fortune." I emphasized the word fortune.

She laughed. Then she said, "What are those voices that I hear in the background? It sounds like a man's voice and a bunch of kids running around."

I paused. My palms started to sweat.

Mom asked, "Are you seeing someone?"

I took a deep breath. "Yes, he's wonderful. His name is Robin, and he is the administrator for a group home on the island. He's from New York; Brooklyn and Queens."

No sooner were the words out of my mouth, did my Dad chime in, apparently listening on the second line. "Is he from New York or from the Islands?" He asked with a sarcastic tone of voice.

I saw where this was going. I lowered my voice. "Robin's working here at the group home, helping his mother who is a minister for the Salvation Army. He was working in Boston and is on a sabbatical from MIT. He's incredibly smart." I was sure to emphasize the word smart.

My dad's voice grew louder. "Is he Black? He better not be Black. He better not be from the islands." He ranted on unintelligibly and continued to chastise me on the phone.

I started to cry silently because I knew he would never accept Robin, or me for loving Robin.

I heard my mom in the background. "Jack, Jack, calm down. It's okay."

"No, Daddy, he's from New York, and he's not Black." My fists balled up in anger. I felt the loss of control. I wanted to slam the phone down on him. As soon as the words were out of my mouth, I had a vision of the next few years. It was a vision of lies, or worse yet, the vision of truth.

Several years later, Robin and I returned to Boston from St. Thomas, after spending several months unwinding in New York City. We were starting to plan a wedding for July of 1985. I was excited about tying the knot, but the memory of my phone conversation years earlier still haunted me. By this point I had not spoken to my parents in several months.

I gave it a feeble attempt. I called Mom to let her know we were planning a wedding. I asked her to come to Boston to help. She reluctantly accepted the invitation. I knew that she lied to my dad.

I picked Mom up from Logan Airport in June. It was her intention to spend a few days with me at my apartment. I wanted to introduce her to Robin for the first time, but I felt overwhelmed and nervous at the very thought. I was unsure of the outcome. We had plans to meet Robin at a Legal Seafood restaurant in downtown after Mom came back to the house to drop off her suitcase.

I waved to her as she got off of the plane. I was stunned. I hadn't seen her for almost two years, and I thought she looked great. The last time we got together was when Kathy and I came to Florida to visit my parents at their new condo in Delray Beach.

She hugged me and called me "Nanettey," her endearing nickname for me. I breathed in her scent of bath salts and baby powder. For a moment, I almost got lost in her shoulder, but she pulled away, and we continued walking out of the terminal, chatting nervously.

When we got to the apartment in downtown Boston where Robin and I lived, she looked around and smiled. I wondered if she thought that I lived in a tenement or something.

We quickly got her organized, and I let her know that I would sleep on the large sofa so she could have the queen bed. She seemed to relax a bit. I kept my fingers crossed.

We drove through the narrow streets and parked directly in front of the entrance of Legal Seafood. As I got out of the car, I saw Robin waiting for us inside the restaurant. My heart flipped twice and my stomach rolled over. This was going to be a test.

Robin opened the door for us and as soon as we were inside, he said, "Mother, it is so good to finally meet you. I'm Robin, but my birth name is Robert. Feel free to call me Robin."

My mother shook his hand. During dinner, I watched for any fatal signs that everything had gone south, but there were none. I monopolized the conversation, talking rapidly, as to leave no space for any unwanted questions.

Robin charmed my mother, with every spoken word so it seemed. They chatted about New York, New York University, and Queens, where he was born. All the while, I sat there nervously picking at my nails or biting my lip. I wasn't hungry at all.

Finally, lunch came to a close. Robin walked back to his workplace, and Mom and I ventured out into the city to find a wedding dress. As we browsed around in a few stores, I could tell her energy level and temperament were changing. She seemed to have lost interest and focus in why we were there. I saw a cute dress that I thought would be a perfect match for me, but as soon as I mentioned that I was going to try it on, she claimed she had a horrible headache, and wanted to return to the townhome. This was the harbinger I dreaded. This was my moment of truth. My vision realized.

We walked back to the car, barely talking, and then drove the two miles to my apartment.

Once we got inside and sat down, I could tell she wasn't comfortable any longer. She kept twitching and sighing. She asked if she could use my phone to call my dad. I walked into the bathroom and ran water to avoid listening to a conversation I knew all too well.

Several minutes went by, and she called my name. She said, "Nanette, I'm not feeling well at all. My head is spinning and I think I need to go home."

I said, "Home? Do you mean to Florida?" I started to panic. She replied, "Yes. I need to fly back home now."

She touched the top of her chest and began to cry. "I'm so sorry, I'm so sorry, Nanette. It's getting me all upset right now and I feel very sick in my stomach and dizzy. I want to go home."

I asked her if she wanted to spend the night. I wanted her to stay so badly. It was what mothers and daughters did while planning a wedding, like shopping for my dress, or picking out special flowers. She said it was impossible. With that being said, we called and got her a flight reservation for eight o'clock that evening.

I called Robin at his job. He couldn't believe what transpired over a matter of four hours. He drove us all to the airport in silence. When we walked Mom to the gate, she hugged and kissed me, and gave a small hug to Robin. As I let go of her hand, she slowly walked toward the gate, turned her head around and said, "I'll see you in July," even though I knew it was a lie.

Robin and I were married in July of 1985 without her or my dad. Case closed.

2. When I saw Mom in Fair Oaks of Delray.

Mom used to lament that she had mental illness. She felt that she inherited it from her father's side of the family. She never got over seeing her dad taken away in a straightjacket. She told me that she felt lost and abandoned when he left and never came back.

I felt the same way when she ended up in Fair Oaks several months following my dad's death. After my mom wrote a note indicating that she didn't want to live anymore, her family doctor insisted that she go to see a psychiatrist, Dr. Eckers, a local doctor in Delray. At first, she went for counseling and talked about many things. Many of those things she kept close to her heart, and I was not privy to them. But I knew she was suffering from depression and the disease we call loneliness. It got the best of her.

Before I knew what had happened, my Aunt Mickey called to tell me that Mom was admitted to Fair Oaks of Delray on the advice of her psychiatrist. She resided in the facility where she received counseling and pharmaceutical treatment for close to three months. I knew it couldn't be easy. My imagination wandered to dark places, as I thought about her frail body and mind, trying to find a place to feel secure. I thought about how my grandmother refused to accept my mom for all of her accomplishments and simply ignored her. I felt sad.

The worst possible day was when Aunt Mickey and I made a trip to visit Mom. We could only stay one hour and have lunch with her. The first thing my mom did was to show me her room, a small private getaway in a very sterile environment. It looked well taken care of and the staff was accommodating. Even though the nurses did not walk around sporting starched uniforms or carry cattle prods, visions of old movies awaited me at every turn.

Mom talked mostly about a friend of hers, another senior woman in her condo complex, who had depression after her husband passed away. However, her depression was clinically severe and she needed shock treatments. Hearing this made me feel scared as I would never have allowed that for my mom. Our short visit finally came to a close, and mom was able to escort us to the side door. There were big windows everywhere and I was able to see her as we closed the door behind us and started to walk down the hallway. Mom rapped on the window, and when I looked back, she held up her right arm, showing me the special watch that I gave her for Mother's Day, several months before. She raised her hand high over and over as if to say, I'm here, I'm here, I have the watch you gave me, as she pointed to it. She mouthed, "I love you."

I cried the whole way driving back to my Aunt Mickey's condo, as she tried to offer soothing and comforting words. I cried because I couldn't bear to see my mom so disfranchised and in a mental hospital. I wanted to rescue her, but luckily for all of us, she made a comeback, shortly thereafter.

The memory of her holding up the watch, staring wide-eyed out the glass window, has left an indelible memory on my psyche, one that I will never forget.

3. My parents went on vacation and changed the locks on the house so I couldn't get in.

I knew it was time to leave. Daddy and I were hating each other, and my mother did nothing to make it better. I felt as if I had no other options but to go. All Daddy ever cared about were my teeth. How I looked. How I made him look. I wanted to be a normal college student. Hell, I made great grades, top of the class, eager to go to school. But that wasn't good enough for either of my parents.

I still had to follow strict rules at eighteen. I introduced my mother to Ted. I knew she didn't like him. I take that back. She would have loved him if it wasn't for the fact that he wasn't Jewish. It didn't matter that he was kind, good-looking, hard-working, and smart. He had options in life, although his upbringing was challenging and his family was odd. Maybe that got in the way of her liking him. Who knows?

I took the plunge that I was waiting for. The job I didn't finish when I was in grade school. I ran away again. Only this time, I succeeded. I packed my things in five paper grocery bags the night before and stored them in my closet. I called Ted and we set the plan. He would pick me up at the house, around back, soon after you went to work. Dinner was as usual. Cleanup followed. I kissed my parents good-night and went into my bedroom. I turned on my T.V. and cried softly into my comforters. I really didn't want to do this. I knew it would break my heart, but it was too late. I barely slept, with ideas that my parents thought tomorrow was just going to be another day. Breakfast, shower, drive to work.

When ten o'clock in the morning rolled around, I was pacing nervously. I told Ted to go to the back door of the house, park on the side, and enter through the side gate, which I left unlocked. I didn't want any nosy neighbor finding out what was going on. While I waited for him to show up, I carefully placed the runaway note on the kitchen table. I knew my mom would find it sooner or later. She knew I had a long day at college.

Ted arrived safely and helped me load the bags in the car. I started to cry again. He reassured me that everything was going to be okay. I wanted to believe him. We wanted to be together. I really did love him.

We drove away in his refurbished 1968 Chevy. We headed toward the Southern State Parkway and drove the short distance to his home in Hempstead, Long Island. Before we got there, I realized I forgot something of importance, the small gold and sapphire necklace that Mom gave me for my seventeenth birthday. I had to go back to get it. Ted drove us all the way back to my house. I checked to see if anyone was there and ran back inside to get the jewelry. I was out in a flash. By this time, I was feeling nervous and more emotional. Another cry. I thought of my best friend, Laura, who lived nearer the highway. I told Ted that I wanted to say something to her. He agreed to swing by for just a moment.

As we were nearing the corner of her home, I saw my mother, sitting on the little bench on Laura's lawn. I couldn't believe what I was seeing. I saw her crying with her head in her hands. She looked terrible. She didn't see me, but she was close enough to hear me if I had yelled out the window.

Oh, my God, I thought, she came looking. She's searching for me, not believing I left. She must have read the note. She must have come back to the house right after we left. I yelled at Ted to get out of there before she saw me, and he spun around. With my eyes flooded with tears, a huge weight bearing down on my chest, we drove back to Ted's home without speaking.

When we opened the front door to the house, I was greeted by his mother, Stella, who was in a drunken stupor. It was going to be a long night, and I was starting to wonder if this was such a good idea after all.

A few days later, I called my mom from Ted's house, reassuring her that I wasn't kidnapped or in jail, or anything that may have entered her mind, as I did leave a note explaining all of what was going on.

We spoke for only fifteen minutes. I could make out my father's rants in the background, but Mom was sniffling as she spoke. It was a very tender moment. There was only clarity, not confrontation. Mom spoke softly, and then we said our goodbyes. I would talk with her again in a few days to a week, after I sorted things out.

After the last phone conversation that my mom and I had, five or six weeks went by without us speaking to each other by phone. I assumed my mom was busy with the store, and she probably thought I had vanished from the face of the earth. In this time, I reflected on what I had done, and still held fast to the fact that the only option was to remove myself from the toxic situation. I decided to pay my parents a visit and showed up at their house unannounced. It was technically still my house as well, since my room and all of its furniture and many of my tchotchkes remained behind. I anticipated the conversation with them as a skittish one, because of all of the time gone by, but I didn't in my wildest dreams anticipate what happened next.

I pulled up in the long driveway, close to the garage, surprised to see that no car was in the driveway, especially since it was a Sunday. They rarely went out. I rang the doorbell and waited. No answer. I rang again. Still no answer. I knocked loudly with the knocker. No response. I started to worry if everyone inside was all right. I thought to myself that they may have gone out for a bite to eat or long drive. I opened my purse, and pulled out my keys. On the whimsical pewter unicorn key ring, still sat my original house key. I put the key in the lock, and I froze.

The key did not open the lock.

I tried turning it every which way and wiggling it into the lock. It refused to open the door. I walked around the house and into the side gate to the back door. I tried the key again in the new lock. Not a chance. The door didn't budge.

After many attempts with no results, I realized they weren't home. But, where was the car? They only had one at this point in time, so I used the key to enter the garage door. It still didn't work, except that I could peer through the narrow window. I realized that my parent's metallic Cadillac Eldorado was tucked away in the neat garage. What the hell?

I sat on the back stoop and thought about what I could do. Finally, I realized I had to find someone in the neighborhood. Someone had to know where my parents went. My Nanny and Aunt Claire, Mom's sister, lived several miles away, but they were totally unaware that I had left home. Calling them would have opened up a huge can of worms, not to mention upsetting my grandmother. So, I strolled across the street and knocked on Mary's door. Mary and her husband were good friends of my parents. They were shocked to see me standing there and even more shocked when I asked them, "Mary, Jim, did my parents go away somewhere?"

I lied to them when I said, "I was out of town and was going to surprise them with a visit. They didn't know I was coming."

Mary laughed and said, "It's good to see you, Nanette. Your mom said you were at college and living with a friend closer to school. Makes sense. Anyway, yeah, they did go away. They went to Jamaica and another island, uh, not sure which one. I think they said they would be gone for three weeks. But they only left about three days ago." She continued on, "Is there anything Jim and I can do for you?"

I thought for a moment. Then I said, "Actually there is. I can't find my key. Did they happen to leave a spare with you?"

"No," Mary replied, "but they hid a key under a planter in the back yard. Go check it out."

I thanked them both and trotted back to the house. Sure, enough, there was the key like they said. I grabbed it and tried the back door once again.

Voila! It worked. At first, I felt like a burglar in a movie. A bit of mystery. But then, as I opened the door all of the way and stepped into the kitchen, I felt sad, devastated. My parents had locked me out of my own home. My favorite comforter still lingered on my bed. My pictures in frames on the dresser showed happy faces on the outside. Clearly, I wasn't wanted back. They treated me as if I was a common thief. That after months of being gone, separated from the only parents I knew, they didn't trust me enough to let me back into my own home. They didn't even give me the chance to see them again face to face.

As I walked slowly through the house, tears dropping down my face with every turn of a corner, I felt like the stranger once again. The one who didn't belong, ever.

4. I found my dad's gun.

The click of the front door sounded. Locks in place. The sound of crunching potato chips was evident from the den as Dalia, my babysitter, watched a movie. She was a sweet young woman, about eight years older than me. Dalia let me do whatever I wanted. I had the motive and the opportunity.

I was nine years old when I began searching. I lied to Dalia and told her that I wanted to get my dolly from the bedroom. I had searched everywhere. Not for the dolly, but for me. I was looking for evidence of me at nine years old.

I began in my parents' bedroom, off-limits unless they were present. First I looked under the bed, only to find old shoes and junk that my mom didn't want to haul up to the attic. As I crawled on my hands and knees along the large area rug, I felt like a detective from a movie who was on the hunt for a criminal. I felt like a criminal, disobeying my father and lurking in my parents' room without their permission, while Dalia watched television.

I spotted the heavy nightstand door. It was slightly ajar and caught my attention. I could smell my dad's side of the bed, hints of Mennen foot powder on the rug. I hated that smell. It reminded me of his power over me.

I pulled open the ornate door with care, and inside I saw magazines piled high. I threw them aside and thought, I'll look through those later. Why I wanted to do that, I didn't know. Maybe I was trying to get an inside glimpse into my father's life.

My eyes got wide with fear, my heart raced in my chest, and my palms felt sweaty, as my hand felt something inside the cabinet. I felt a handle. I pulled it out. It was a gun. It was my dad's gun. I had watched enough westerns to know the difference. I sat cross-legged on the floor running my hands along the gun. It felt cold and smooth in my hands. I saw the leather case, the holster lying beside it. I picked it up and sniffed it. Mennen's powder again. I put the gun back into the cabinet and shoved the magazines around it like it was before.

I wanted to pick up the gun again. I reached for it a second time, and just as I was about to touch the trigger, I heard a noise. It was Dalia on the stairs.

I heard her say, "Nanette, what are you doing up there? Are you alright? Did you find your dolly? Your mom wants you to stay and watch a movie with me. There's ice cream in the fridge. C'mon downstairs now, please."

"Okay," I murmured softly. "I'll be right there."

I slowly laid the gun down where it belonged in my dad's nightstand. I remember how heavy it felt in my tiny hands. When I put the magazines on top of the gun, a piece of paper fell out. It was a picture of a topless woman dressed in a grass skirt with long brown hair. Ugh. That's gross. More Mennen smell.

I covered it all back up and firmly closed the door. I tiptoed out of my parent's room and down the stairs to find Dalia. Halfway down the landing, I remembered that the door was not closed when I found the gun. I wondered if Dad would know I was messing around in his things. I didn't want to think about the consequences. Ice cream took over and I forgot all about it.

When I was a few years older, I learned that the pistol was fully loaded.

5. I crashed a car.

It was the summer of 1973. I had just graduated from high school. I had received my official license to drive—my license to freedom. I was a good driver and passed the test the first time. My father allowed me to drive his Cutlass 442 Olds with beautiful black leather bucket seats and a console to match. He bought the car used but it was in cherry condition. Every so often I would drive it to school or to visit family, but I knew he was worried sick about what would happen to this car, his prized possession. In those days, no one locked their car doors.

One afternoon, as I drove down Brookville Boulevard, a street which connected Nassau and Queens, I paused at a traffic light just under the highway overpass. Traffic was coming in several directions.

My light was red. I stopped, of course, and waited. The light turned green and I tapped the gas.

Within seconds, a car slammed into my passenger side. The car must have come off the highway ramp or maybe the lights were out of sync. I didn't have a moment to think or ask questions before my car lurched forward and I was barreling down Brookville Boulevard toward JFK Airport at record speed. The accelerator pedal was stuck to the floor.

I was frantic. I was hitting the brakes with gusto, but they only grinded, and smoky air filled the car through the open windows. I was sweating from the heat and my heart beat wildly, as I continued to slam my foot into the brake with little resolve, noticing people coming toward me on the opposite side of the street. They were flashing their lights and screaming obscenities out the window. My car window was down and I could hear the intense grinding from the brakes. As I continued to hurtle down the busy street, hanging onto the large steering wheel with all of my might, I started to shake violently and realized that I could die if the car didn't stop.

With that thought rumbling in my head, I did the only thing I could do. I had to stop the car and prevent further carnage. I couldn't run over people on the sidewalk or take a chance that I might cause a major accident at the next big intersection. If I drove too much further, I would've crashed into the far end of Kennedy Airport and landed in a ditch underwater.

I turned the car toward a street pole alongside a small park, reached down, and threw the gears into park, hearing the awful twisting sounds of the transmission disengaging and dismantling. I closed my eyes, gripped the wheel, and hurtled straight into the pole. Bam! The car lurched, and my body lunged forward, narrowly missing the windshield. My lap belt wasn't much help.

When I looked up, I realized the car was on fire under the hood. Through the open driver's side window, I saw people getting out of their cars. Without thinking, I pulled the key out of the ignition and threw the keys onto the seat next to me. In a matter of seconds, feeling like I was in a dream, I managed to crawl out of the window, as the door handle wouldn't budge. The engine continued to spew flames.

I was hysterical, screaming and crying and in total disbelief of what just happened. Many bystanders came up to me, offering me water and covering me with shirts or beach towels that they had in their cars.

I saw the ambulance approaching, but my parents were nowhere to be found. Of course, they wouldn't be; no one had called them. The paramedics asked me for my driver license. I sat scared and alone in the company of strangers who were trying to make sense of it all. I could not speak. All I kept thinking about was that when my father arrived, he would crucify me because I wrecked his car. I would be better off dead. I would become a prisoner in my own home, not to mention the shame and disappointment that I would bring upon him. He valued his possession more than he valued me.

When the volunteer fire department rescue team came to talk with me, I didn't want to say anything. What was I going to say? This is the least of the problem? A flaming car with me in it wasn't anything compared to wrecking my dad's pride and joy. They would not understand.

From the corner of my eye, I saw two police officers approach me. They seemed solemn and wanted to find out where my parents were.

"They're at home, sir," I said in a timid voice. I gave them my phone number.

"We're going to call your parents now, Nanette. Is that your name, Nanette?"

"Yes, Nanette Wolf. Please don't tell them that the car went up in flames. Just say that I had a car accident."

"When they get here, we can talk about it, and find out what happened."

"I feel like I'm going to throw up." I spread my feet apart and vomited into the street. I felt like my head was disconnected from my body.

The fire and rescue team waited for my parents to arrive, as they had quickly looked me over and didn't see any burns. I was in shock and badly shaken up, but lucky to be alive. I didn't want to go to the hospital and I let them know that.

"Nanette, oh, my God, Nanette!" I heard my mom's voice. She was frantic and crying as well. "What happened, how did this happen?"

I tried to explain through sobs of my own, but all I wanted to do was hold her and have her stroke my forehead. We both stood there staring at each other, and then my father ran in between us.

"What the hell have you done to my car, you, stupid girl? Do you know that this car was a limited edition, cherry model, one of a kind …?"

The words continued to come out of his mouth as he pointed, gestured, and yelled in my face for at least ten minutes. I bit my bottom lip so hard it bled. Everyone just stood there and stared at this awful scene. The first responders didn't react to my dad's outburst. I wondered if they didn't consider my dad's behavior abusive. I looked over at my mother trying to get her attention. Please help me. Please help me, mommy. Her head was bent down toward the street.

At that consequential moment, when most parents would have been ecstatic and grateful that their child had survived such an accident, coming out with barely a scratch, my parents reacted like the most important thing was a tin box. It may have been a cherry automobile, but they never realized that I was "cherry" too. The child that they wanted. The child that my mother wanted. I thought I was their "chosen" and "special" child. Isn't that what all adopted kids were told? I remembered the look on my parents' face when my teeth were damaged and ruined my looks. I saw the same look on their faces on this day, and felt that I was going to be sent back to the adoption farm.

I felt that I was nothing more than a possession, especially for my father.

When we got home, my mother helped me into the shower, and fed me milk and cookies, just like she did when I was a little girl.

She kissed me good night, and said, "I'm glad you're all right. I love you to the moon and back. I'm sorry that I didn't speak up, Nanette. I just didn't know what to do. Dad gets so mad sometimes, but he does love you."

Mom always seemed to be living with a sense of regret, an awful place to be. I hated my father even more that night and could feel the anger welling up inside me, waiting to explode.

Nat
2000-2007

I HAD JUST begun to re-establish my place in the world with my mother. After my father died and my mother was freed from living his life, she recovered from a major mental breakdown which had landed her in a mental hospital in Delray Beach, Florida. Her days of loneliness and her old depression haunted her, as she wrote in a letter to me.

"Dearest Nanette,

It seems as if I'm looking around and everywhere there is just nothing. The contact between us seems so superficial—we are just mouthing, because it is the thing to do— "I love you I love you"—so what does that mean beyond the words on the telephone. You have made a life—I am happy that it seems to have turned out so well in spite of all obstacles both real and created. Where does that leave me? There is just no room for me there—I must create my own life here, so as it is. I have all the right ingredients but one-ME. I just can't get over the feeling of always being on the fringes neither here nor there. I'm like divided between here and there as if I don't belong anywhere! The Men's Club is having a holiday program and I can't find anyone to go with me. I guess I'll have to go it alone—well I can't have someone holding my hand all of the time and I have to stop running away from the world. Here goes!

Don't be frightened—I'm just letting off steam and mailing it before I chicken out! Love, you"

Signed Mother.

My mother blamed her emotional state on loneliness due to the waning of family attending to her. She explained to me that she felt abandoned by her distant cousin, Bobbie, a woman with whom she had established a good friendship only to have Bobbie leave her flat.

In one of Mom's journals, she writes of her abandonment;

"Friends take all and leave you with nothing; they are not true, but wolves in sheep's clothing. This is a philosophy I developed early on to protect myself from hurt and despair. They have changed me."

Mom and I were left with a new longing for one another. We were just getting started on our journey to becoming closer as mother and daughter, when things came crashing down all over again.

I called her one day after she was released from Fair Oaks Hospital. I was looking forward to planning some of the trips we had talked about taking earlier that year. I called repeatedly with no answer. She didn't own an answering machine. She had no friends I could call. I remarked to Robin how concerned I was. It was not typical of her to venture far from home, particularly after dinner.

After phone contact to Mom proved unsuccessful, I telephoned Aunt Mickey in Ft. Lauderdale. I explained to her that Mom was not picking up the phone and I was worried.

She was just as perplexed, but not worried. "Your mom is probably busy with the Women's Club at the condo," she replied, without a hint of concern.

As I thought more about it, I chalked the whole thing up to the fact that she was just starting to come out of her shell. I saw that the veil of depression had begun to lift. Who was I to judge her social calendar? She was old enough to make her own decisions.

When I finally reached her on the phone the next day, Mom reported that, "I was out with a friend whom I met at a senior citizen's grief seminar." As I began to draw the truth out of her, Mom said that she only dined with a friend.

But, after several weeks of dinners, she picked up her nightgown, toothbrush, and blood pressure medicine. She left her comfortable condo, and went to live with this "friend," whose name was Nat.

Nat was several years older than Mom, and he lived a few blocks away. She seemed to be smitten by him. "He is over six feet tall," she told me, "slender and well-tanned from hours of tennis."

It appeared to me, that at ninety years old, he was everything my father wasn't. After initially getting over the shock of what she told me, I began to think that this was a good idea, and that maybe her loneliness would cease. After one year into the relationship, Nat and my mom became inseparable. No, inseparable is too light of a word to describe what followed. My mother, once again, had lost her nerve, and became the victim of a control freak. He wanted a servant. She needed a companion.

I made attempts to get her to see my point of view. I tried to needle my way into their relationship. I tried to establish my rightful ground as her daughter.

Wasn't I allowed to care about this? Didn't I have a right to try and ensure her safety? Really, who was this guy? My head was filled with all sorts of crazy ideas about what could happen to her. I didn't know much about him, except what my mom told me. He was in his nineties, and he was born in Brooklyn. He had three daughters and one son from whom he was estranged. His wife died around the same time as my dad, and they had been married for sixty years. Now he was lonely.

As my mother become more attached to him, I saw less and less of her. She stopped calling me on a regular basis. At some point, she ceased calling altogether. I was devastated.

She mentioned on several occasions to my cousin Stuart that Nat's family was her real family. Stuart and I reeled with anger at that comment, and it took me a long time to unleash the hurt I felt after that conversation.

Once again, I felt alienated. Abandoned. Given away. I had lost Mother again. I soon fell into panic mode and was desperately seeking my center, whatever the hell that was. My mom and I had plans to spend so much time together.

I thought about all that was supposed to happen now. Our trips were laid out on paper, wherever she desired to go. Robin and my mom had formed a new and wonderful relationship, an acceptance that had him beaming with joy. I thought that she and I were well on our way to talking again, after many years of tension and estrangement. She opened up to me and her sister-in-law, Mickey, about her younger life. She talked more about her marriage to my father. She tried to assert herself in many ways as an individual.

However, Nat's presence at this point put an end to all those dreams and was a harbinger of what was to come.

He did not accept me or Robin. He called him hideous names. He said that Robin was a "nigger" because of Robin's mixed ethnicity. He said I was not my mom's daughter. He believed, like a true paranoid schizophrenic, that Robin and I would take Mom away from him.

In his attempt to secure my mom as a permanent fixture in his life, he treated me with rudeness and rancor, which in turn left my mom with a feeling of helplessness. She often said on a rare phone call, "What can I do, Nanette, I'm alone?" She continued to allow him to be mean.

I felt a replay of the old days as a young child, when my mom stood solid along my dad, no matter what the situation. Good or bad. They were a unit.

I decided to take time away from my job in the hopes of going to see her, even though I knew my time with her would be limited. Mom asked Nat for permission to visit my Aunt Mickey in a nursing home in Ft. Lauderdale, and I accompanied her.

When she and I returned home five minutes late from the visit, Nat opened the front door to his condo and screamed at both of us. The veins in his neck pulsated as he pushed my mother aside, almost making her fall. He lunged at me as his fists balled up in an attempt to hit me. I bolted from his apartment, crying and yelling, as snot ran down my face. I choked back vomit. I was scared of him. I hated him. But most of all, I felt the ultimate loss. Losing my mother. Again.

I drove helter-skelter to a nearby restaurant, where there was a payphone. I dialed a number that I saw in Mom's purse earlier that year. It was for one of his daughters. My mom suggested that I keep it in my wallet for an emergency, in case she and Nat were in an accident. I wanted to throw it away and saw no use for it then. Now, I was glad that I kept it.

I dialed the long-distance number to New Orleans, and Nat's youngest daughter, Charlene, answered the phone. I introduced myself.

"Charlene," I sobbed, "Nat's gone crazy. We had an argument and he tried to push my mom down. He tried to hit me. I think you need to come to Florida. Now."

As I rambled on in between sobs, Charlene tried to calm me down, but I didn't believe that she understood the gravity of the situation. What could she do several hundred miles away? Charlene enlightened me on that short phone call about her early years living with her father. Nat was controlling and strict with Mom; however, I believe that it was hard for Charlene to listen to a situation, which may already have been repeated many times in her life. Now she was hearing it from someone new and unfamiliar to their family.

When I got off the phone almost twenty-five minutes later, I called Robin and recounted the story. He wanted me to come home right away. Ignoring his request, I managed to stay the night at my hotel, and tried to get a few hours of sleep. In the morning, I mustered up the courage to speak with Mom for a few minutes on the phone. She tried to extend a weak apology. I never got one from Nat.

The insane thing about this situation was that I felt as if it was me who was the wrongdoer. Several days later, my mother called and reamed me out for the trouble that I caused between her and Nat. Apparently, Charlene called her father the next day to ask about the "firestorm" that we had. Nat was fuming mad over this, and my mom took his side. She let me know it.

Nat and Mom's relationship was locked tight for close to seven years after that incident. I saw my mom less and less. When I did get the opportunity to visit her, I was limited to a few hours. I had to ask Nat for permission to see her.

I watched my mom's demeanor change, as she struggled with her own demons. Nat was starting to feel the years creep up on him, and Mom was not taking care of herself. It was going to take a true miracle for anything to change. I prayed for sanity. I prayed for love. I prayed for the return of my mother.

Turning the Corner

WHEN NAT DIED in August 2007 it came with a price. I got the miracle that I silently wished for and my mother got heartache.

Several days before he died, he became violently ill and was admitted to a local hospital. Soon after, I received a call late in the evening. It was one of Nat's daughters, Sadie. She insisted that I get on a plane the very next day and come to Nat's bedside. She explained that Nat was in Hospice on his deathbed.

Neither of Nat's daughters were on good terms with me, and it was difficult to talk with them. Sadie explained that I MUST come to the hospital and tell Nat that everything will be okay with my mom and I promise to take care of her. I was offended by what she asked me to do, as I hated him and I believe that she knew that.

Nevertheless, I flew into Delray the next day and went straight to the hospital after checking into the hotel. I called my mom who was surprised that I was in town. I reminded her she told me that Nat was taken to the hospital days earlier and that I wanted to check on her. I never said a word about his grave condition, as the daughters were not expecting her to come to his bedside. In fact, they did not want her there at all. It was only because she suffered from severe vascular dementia, that kept her from getting into her car and driving to see him, which would have been a disaster.

When I arrived at the hospital and was directed towards Nat's room, I was stopped cold by Sadie, who addressed me in an authoritative tone.

"Get over here," Sadie said. "We need to speak with you. What took you so long to get here?" She rambled on. "We expected you much earlier. You didn't discuss this with your mom, did you?"

I was stunned at her outburst and was fuming mad. How dare they speak to me this way. Nat is not my father and he is not my mom's husband. I responded. "I'm sorry, Sadie, but I worked all day at school and had to catch a later flight. I couldn't drive all the way here and still make it. I did the best that I could."

"Well, guess what, your best isn't good enough." She stormed off into an adjacent room.

They asked me to come into a conference room that was set up for families of patients who were in the Hospice Center. For the remaining twenty minutes, which seemed like eternity in hell, I listened to Sadie and Charlene berate me about how I was a bad daughter, why they wanted me here, and how I was going to have to attend to my mother. With clenched teeth, I quoted to myself a popular expression, "the beatings will continue…until morale improves."

I got up and walked down the hall into Nat's room. He looked dead to me. He was dead to me. I shut the door to the room. I approached the bed and stared at his lifeless form. The blankets were pulled close to his neck, and all I saw was his head. The red-tan face with evidence of skin cancer was no longer there. It was replaced with a pallor reserved for vampires. That he was. He sucked the life out my mother, and I was his second victim. He said he loved her and would protect her. He didn't want to be alone, yet he robbed me of my role as daughter.

I got closer and whispered into his ear.

"My mother thought you would cure her loneliness. But, you may have. You were just like my dad, controlling, insensitive and, selfish. I promise that my mother will be fine without you. I love her more than you will ever know and I will take care of her more than you ever could."

"I hate you Nat."

"But, I forgive you."

"Goodbye," I whispered.

I walked out of Nat's room and headed for the elevator. I had to get some sleep. Tomorrow I would have to tell my mom that Nat died. I got the call at one in the morning stating that Nat had actually passed away.

When I awoke in the hotel room the following morning, I could barely stand up. My body and mind felt bruised beyond repair and I felt depressed. I had a big job ahead of me.

Charlene wanted me to tell Mom the truth. I showered, slammed down some food at a local eatery and drove to Nat's condo where Mom was staying. I gave a rap on the door and she appeared, looking dazed as usual, but dressed in a newer outfit. As soon as I entered the small living room, my mom's lower lip began to quiver. With tears in my eyes for her, I announced that Nat passed away and that his heart gave out.

"After all, he was almost ninety-seven years old," I told her.

Before I could get all of the words out, she let out a moan and fell into the seat of the couch. I sat down next to her and she cried steadily into my shoulder. My heart broke for her and her loss, although I still hated him.

My thoughts turned to months down the road, and what I was going to do to make things better for her. I held her tight and rocked her against my body as if she was a child. I could not bear to see my mother in this condition.

It was decided in early October of 2007, that my mom was to be moved from Nat's apartment to her own condo, which she still owned. Part of the decision was due to the fact that Nat's daughter, Charlene, wanted to sell the unit and wanted Mom out of there, pronto. It seemed more like an eviction to me. Neither one of Nat's daughters really cared for my mother, any more than a bear likes humans. It became clear to me at that time, that they had used my mother to fill the void in Nat's life after the sudden death of his wife several years before. They pretended to befriend Mom to the point that she thought they were her family.

We sat at Sadie's dining room table, and my mom was handed a stack of papers to sign, saying that she could live in the apartment for a month, and then everything that was hers had to be removed. Mom didn't realize the impact of those papers, but I vowed never to speak with Nat's people again.

They didn't love her. She was convenient, and filled a purpose. Months after she passed away, looking through some important papers, I came across her checkbooks. The grand total of approximately seven thousand dollars was Mom's contribution to Nat's income and household, which she gave with no regrets or strings attached. There was no trace of any formal agreement, but in any case, she was asked to leave.

Several weeks later, help was on the way.

Robin and I showed up one day in late October ready to do the impossible. We were moving Mom back to her condo in Delray Beach.

She was finally being rescued from the one place that a recent *Sun Sentinel* newspaper article deemed "the most depressing and lonely place to live in Palm Beach County. It is where people go to die." The article may have been right, but not for my mom. She was never going to die there or any place else, so I thought. My mom had her own plans.

As Robin cleaned and scrubbed the filthy, worn out apartment, Mom and I headed to the bank and ran various errands to secure her finances.

As I sat and listened to what the bank manager had to say, I looked over at her, and the veil of dementia was pulled as far down as a woolen cap on a cold winter's day. She had nothing left to give, and I was just beginning to understand, yet not knowing, how or what it would take to help her, even for a little while.

Finally, after two intense days of hard physical labor, and mentally enduring all of the questions my mom repeatedly asked us, she was settled back into her own condo, which she and my dad had shared for thirty years.

It seemed so different than I remembered. It was cleaner than I have ever witnessed it, due in part to the wonderful efforts of Vera and Luis. They were the wonderful couple who we hired to restore Mom's place to a livable space. This couple completed a task that would normally take weeks or more and finished the job in seventy-two hours. I thank God to this day for both of them, and I hope wherever they are, that they knew how much Mom appreciated them.

I knew how fearful Mom was of returning here, even though we begged her to return to St. Pete with us. She wanted me to spend the night. Jesus Christ, I just couldn't do it. I could not be with the only real mother I had, for a measly twenty-four hours. I didn't have the emotional strength for the sadness she displayed. It was torture for me. At the same time, I blamed her for all of the old mistakes she made, and I couldn't let it go. We loved each other from a distance. It was a little game we played. I hated it.

There was no doubt, I was damaged because of it.

Any decent daughter would have obliged and realized the impending outcome. Instead, Robin and I retreated back to the hotel like scared rabbits. It was our home away from home.

My thoughts plagued me over and over. What was going to happen to Mom now? How could she do all of the things that she had to do by herself? She still drove (the scariest thought ever) but that needed to change as well.

In spite of all of my worrying, Mom's first two nights in her "new" home seemed to go well. She still pined for Nat or was it for loss in general? She never was able to grieve for my father years before, why should she grieve for Nat now?

At the end of a tireless week, Robin and I packed up, assured by Mom that she would be fine. She thanked us one million times for helping her. Although an omnipresent shroud of guilt surrounded me, the next few months seemed to pass with little incident. I retreated to the security of my classroom, with a renewed sense of passion for my students.

My mother was still alone.

Several months went by, and repeated trips were made out of duty, honor and love for my mother. Just before her ninety-second birthday, things changed for the worst. The condominium office was calling my job on a regular basis to report incidences of how my Mom was repeatedly showing up at wrong apartments or getting locked out of her own.

The neighbors that she had known for many years all watched with frightful eyes as Mom carried heavy grocery bags one at a time up the stairs to her condo. Today, as I recall it, the pain of this vision is just as potent as it was back then. How did she do this day after day, I will never know, but it still breaks my heart to imagine what was true.

"Bad day at Black Rock," as Mom would have said.

As we showed up at her door to celebrate this esteemed birthday, several months after her arrival back to her home, Mom was excited to see us and Mia, our Shih-Tzu, in tow. She could not have been more grateful. The look on her face and her shrunken body in rag-tag clothes was a telling moment for both Robin and me.

Even though Vera and Luis came bi-monthly to clean, they could not attend to the dirty, smelly underwear in her hamper, stained with week old urine and feces. It was sad to see the bathroom towels that never got used or the moldy containers of half-eaten tuna fish in the frig.

Once we settled in and encouraged her to try on her new outfits, a small glimmer of hope became apparent. She paraded around the bedroom in the outfit, looking like a million bucks.

"Wow, Mom, you look great!" I said. This was the Harriet Wolf I was used to seeing.

As the coolness of the South Florida winter settled in like a refreshing Popsicle, the end of a new school semester was rapidly approaching, and I was getting a much-deserved break. There was no question in my mind how I was going to spend it.

Several months later on a return visit, I met with the gentleman from the Buick dealership. We were selling Mom's 1993 Buick Le Sabre with forty-six thousand miles. This was the last car that she and my dad owned together. This object, like everything else, was going to the graveyard. Even with the low mileage, the car needed major repairs. After numerous collisions, due to my mom's impaired driving habits and lack of oil, the car had seen better days. As I took the six-hundred-dollar check from the dealer's hands, I knew he was doing both of us a favor, and he cheerily waved a goodbye to Mom, who was peering down from the doorway with the distinct look of Black Rock on her face. I saw the teardrops fall from her beautiful green eyes, and she managed to utter "end of an era." What she really meant was the end of her.

Not long after the car was sold, we sat on her sticky and stained tan couch in the den for hours, without many words spoken between us. Eventually, she started to ask questions about the car, forgetting that it was sold. I tried to be gentle in my tone, but the invasive and persistent dementia-style questioning was nagging at me, and I tried desperately to change the topic.

Fortunately for both of us, the remainder of the visit panned out to be promising. Mom seemed to accept the loss of the car more and more, and it was almost time for me to go home. The refrigerator was stocked for at least ten days, and she knew how to call a cab for a trip to the grocery store for replacements. Even with continual and persistent prodding to come live in our area at a "nice" assisted living facility, or a small apartment around the corner from our home, she dug her heels in and insisted that she would make it. I was not sure who she was trying to reassure more, her or me.

The weeks ahead into the new semester of January 2008 were jammed packed with school activities and life at home. Mom called every single day, and we established a time for our daily communication. I was trying feverishly to enroll her in the Mae Volen Center in Delray Beach, a senior citizen gathering place. As I juggled my work responsibilities, I managed to contact the various elder health agencies and making my first attempt at seeking a Hospice counselor for myself. I was going to need it sooner than later, but I knew now was the time. This last visit with my Mom prompted me to act as if on fire, as I glanced down at her elephant legs ballooned with blue veins pushing against her pale and flaky dry skin. Her green eyes were beautiful, but the fluid filled pouches that surrounded them spoke of something very wrong and very sickly. Although I made several calls a week to her primary care physician, nothing seemed to improve. My mother's calendar was filled with doctor's appointments ranging from cardiologists to podiatry to general blood pressure checkups, yet no one noticed the signs of major illness? I was listening to her complaints with a daughter's ear and all I heard was "I am going to die soon."

That's when the call to the Mae Volen Center was made.

It was one year later that I found a piece of balled up newspaper in one of Mom's messy closets. When I unfolded it, staring me right in the face, like a blast of hot air, were the scratched-out words, "Mae Volen" along with their telephone number. My heart truly broke that day, and I fell down on my knees sobbing uncontrollably. She had made a desperate call to help herself.

Angel Mary
2008

I NEEDED HELP in a bad way. My mother was dying and I couldn't stop it.

I didn't know how to help her. It was one of those moments when I wanted to pack myself into a suitcase and leave everything behind, including my mother. I offered her many opportunities to live near Robin and me, but she refused. I called assisted living facilities on a daily basis, hoping for the perfect one that would take my mother. She refused over and over again.

Finally, I landed a phone call with a woman who seemed caring and responsible. She worked for a reputable assisted living facility in Delray Beach, called the Mae Volen Center. It serviced the elderly in many capacities and offered daycare, where my mom could play cards, talk with other women and possibly meet a friend. All things she used to love.

It was a miracle that she agreed to go there, and once Mom heard that a bus would pick her up, she gave the go-ahead. I thought I was saved from the burden and guilt of caring for her.

Several weeks went by as she called daily to report on her experiences. Mom liked the surroundings at first, but I could hear the truth in her voice, and I knew better than to believe her.

I got calls the following week from the caring facility.

"You need to come get your mother," the voice on the other end said multiple times. "She's wandering away and almost left the parking lot. We can't have a resident who has dementia."

You bitch, I thought to myself, it's your responsibility to see that she stays put. And my mother does not have dementia, I lied to myself.

Several days later, they refused her entry to the center, and claimed she was unfit for their services. No one returned a single phone call to explain why. Everyday thereafter, until days before she died, my mother still questioned why they wouldn't take her, and I couldn't give her a reason. I felt as though I had failed her in every way.

Exactly one month after the Mae Volen debacle, a woman responded to our pleas for help regarding mom's care. At the time, I didn't realize that she would have wings. This woman came from a local agency called Senior Home Companions, which was run by one of the most competent and compassionate people on earth, Gloria. After much discussion on the phone, it was decided by Gloria and me, that Mary, her caregiver-to-be, was supposed to provide non-medical companionship and light housekeeping duties.

This was a self-pay service, and it took a good deal of convincing on my part to assure my mom that this woman was not going to rob her blind or gag her and run. She was initially hired to come three days per week, and add more time as needed. At first, progress was slow and after Mary left my mom's house daily, Mom would call me to give a full report complaining about this or that. As I sat on my garden porch trying to achieve some moments of peace and solitude, I gritted my teeth and thought to myself, "What more do you want, stop being such a pain, just let the woman do what she is there to do." My level of exasperation, combined with fear and heartbreak at hearing her lament, ate at me every day like a parasite.

After one week, Mary called me to formally introduce herself. It was while she was officially still "on duty," and she remarked that the conversation would be short. As I listened to her voice, calm and even, I heard a "Mrs. Doubtfire" quality. The quiet, steady rhythm of her conversation, combined with a hint of a royal British accent, instantly soothed me. I grimaced as I heard my mom shouting loudly in the background and giving instructions to Mary as to what to say. Poor Mary. I pulled the phone away from my ear and thought, this isn't going well. I was apparently wrong, very wrong.

The long and short of it was that Mary turned out to be the best thing in the world for my mom, fulfilling all of her elder person needs and then some. The part that I didn't see at the time was what she was doing for me. Little did I know, that in six months' time, the only mother I had was going to leave me for good this time, and I was going to return to my original state of orphan-dom. The only thing that I believed and still do, was when that first phone call was made and Mary accepted the job, that a universal force was at work, and God himself knew that I was going to need Mary months and years from then.

I continue to recall how Mary sat by my mother's beside at Hospice, and how she soothed and distracted both my mom and me with her delightful laugh and hilarious stories of her early years as an Eastern flight attendant.

As Mary and Mom would carry out their days together, tooling around Delray Beach in Mary's silver Toyota Corolla, with the little tennis ball wavering on the antennae, I heard and saw a whole new mom. Our conversations seemed brighter, replacing the old complaining and silence that always seemed to be present. She routinely replied, "Mary is great." A total transformation was taking place, with Mary as the conduit between us.

For the next two to three months that followed, my mom talked up a storm with every conversation. She had a good deal to say, and I lingered on every word as if it were her last. Each ring of the phone, bearing her name on the caller ID, gave me cause to snatch up the line, waiting to hear her voice. I am not sure why I felt the way I did, but I loved my mother more than ever during this time, and more than I could voice to anyone. I needed her so badly then, to hug and hold me, to rub the long-remembered Pacquin's lotion on my hands, to be the mother she always wanted to be, and I the daughter I could have been.

As we talked at length day after day about many things, I rubbed my hands together and could smell the aroma of the hand cream on my hands, taking me back to way better times. She revealed herself completely and wholly to me, and I often found the honesty difficult to bear. "Why couldn't we communicate like this before?" I asked myself. The love was pouring out of her, and Mary was helping her do this in an insidious way. My mom was thankful, I know, for all of the trips to the beauty parlor that Mary afforded her, and the weekly treks to the local pizzeria for a "great slice." The last time I recall my mom eating pizza was in 1965 at the California Pizza Place, located in the Green Acres Mall in our home town of Valley Stream, New York.

What was happening here, I thought to myself. My mom was finally living for a change, being herself, freedom at last.

I hold the belief that Mary encouraged her to say what she felt in her heart.

One day, while fully engaged in our daily talks, my mom nonchalantly asked, "Nanette, were you ever jealous of Nat and me?" My silence, which must have seemed like an eternity, did not make her suspicious, and out of respect for her feelings, I answered very softly in my usual way, "No, Mom, not at all, why would you think that?" She did not come back with a reply, but I knew better, and being my mom, she knew my real answer.

For the first time in fifty years, she was giving me the opportunity to be myself. She allowed me to bare my true feelings to her, without guilt, fear, anguish, or worry about whether she liked the reply or not. However, I felt ashamed after she asked me that question about Nat, because I couldn't be honest enough with myself to reveal what my heart felt inside about him. Maybe I wasn't strong enough.

It wasn't until several years after her death that I began my mornings with a new ritual of truth for myself: to declare to her out loud everything I was thinking, past and present. I received the gift of acceptance from her each day.

With spring rapidly approaching, I began to covet the meaning of renewal, of cleansing, of a new beginning. I experienced love in a new-found way. Each phone call, every moment spent visiting Mom, was dedicated to us being whole again. During this time of extra care and reflection, I regretted that she and I never went on a real vacation. I wanted to take her somewhere faraway or exotic, the way she and my dad traveled the world. I always wanted to ask her, but was afraid that she would say "no."

Mary continued to contact me by phone to inform me of Mom's progress, which by late April of 2008, was not looking positive. Her spirits were remaining high, but her body and mind were failing. She reported that it was of the utmost importance that I contact a new doctor. Mary witnessed the continual decline as she watched my mom's legs swell up to gigantic proportions. The podiatrist felt he could no longer attend to her issues and he ceased treating her with the exception of a pedicure.

I spent most of my days at school, calling different doctors on my forty-five-minute planning periods. There was no one who offered a solution, other than to say she is "getting old." I had to hold my breath each time I heard that, for fear that I would become undone and unleash a verbal fury.

The true realization of how our elders are treated in this society took my faith away that year, and spawned a unique anger in my heart, one that I certainly wasn't used to. I pushed that feeling aside and vowed that at a later date, I would become more involved with the plight of the elderly. If only her fellow humans, people dedicated to truly healing the sick, could take a moment out of their "busy" schedules and just listen to mom. Please roll up her pants and take a look at those ankles and see the jiggled Jell-O eyes, I screamed to myself, out of sheer frustration.

At that point I didn't give a damn how many patients her doctor saw, this was MY mother, and she needed help. I finally recoiled realizing that I was wasting my time with these people. I lost faith in the Hippocratic Oath.

As Mary continued her compassionate outreach and made life better for us, Robin and I made another pilgrimage to see her for Mother's Day that year. L'il Mia was with us, which gave a bit of uplift to mom. She loved to stroke her soft fur and allowed Mia to burrow into her chest. Mia squirmed with delight. Robin made his usual jokes and we celebrated in grand style taking some of the pain away, if only for a short while. All three of us indulged in pizza in our regular room at the Residence Inn on the beach.

As I sat shoulder to shoulder with Mom on the couch, we held hands tightly, her misshapen fingernails curled around mine. I continued to watch the faraway gaze along with smelling the biting odor of stale urine. I faced the tormented reality that this was going to be the last Mother's Day we would spend together on this planet. Indeed, it was.

Last Days

MY MOTHER, HARRIET Bressler Wolf died at 12:20 P.M. on Monday, June 16, 2008. I was not there to comfort her or hold her hand as she passed away.

As I look back on all of those tenuous years, I realized how much I learned about real love, sacrifice, bravery, and courage, and how one person could be saved over and over again by the love of one other person, my mother. My life story has been about just that: one orphan's tale of inspiration, hope, and survival, and taking the longest road on earth to realize that love does exist in a place where once thought lost.

The word "infection" permeated my thoughts as my husband, Robin, and I received a call from the Hospice nurse on Saturday stating that she was going downhill in a hurry and we should consider making our way to the facility. On the day before this disturbing call, I remember getting ready for my friend, Jean's, visit.

I was upstairs in the hall closet cleaning out some old files and making room for her weekend-long stay. I knew how sick my mom was, and I had made repeated trips to see her in the last month which was eating into my psyche and depleting any energy I had left. I wanted to disappear into the sea of files and never come out. Jean was going to be the perfect distraction.

I replied to the nurse on the phone, "I will be there on Monday morning."

She replied, "Are you sure?" I could hear the disappointment in her voice.

"Yes, Monday," I confirmed. What was I thinking? My mother was dying, and I glibly had told the nurse, "I will be there tomorrow." Why was I so afraid of more telling words between her and me? Her condition was worsening, and I didn't even give her the dignity of being there to hold her hand and to help her get through this difficult period.

The day flew by and I distracted myself with Jean's lighthearted presence, as if it would keep my mother from dying. We ate masses of chocolate brownies, commented on how we could fix the world's problems, and laughed about old sweethearts until we climbed into bed. Jean was offering her support as I prepared to enter the 2008 Madeira Beach Mad Dog Triathlon at 7:00 a.m. the following morning.

I got up that Sunday morning, totally focused on the race ahead in the sweltering heat and humidity. I didn't think once about my mother. When I could no longer take the heat, I dug my heels into the soft sand, trying to finish the 3.5-mile end of the race. With each heel strike, I moaned and let out guttural sounds. Sounds of heat exhaustion, sounds of pain, and sounds of grief, as I pounded it all out of me onto that hot sand.

When I went to bed Sunday night, after Jean drove home, my first thought was that my mother, who saved me so many years ago, always promised me that she was never going to die, let alone in a nursing home which smelled of urine and bad mistakes. I was letting her down big time.

The following morning, Robin and I headed out to make the four-hour drive to Delray. As we made the turn to get on the Sawgrass Expressway from I-95, I could feel my mom calling out to me, begging me to hurry.

My cell phone rang. When I answered, the Hospice pastor asked, "Is this Nanette? She spoke in a low, hushed tone. "Your mom just passed away."

"Noooooooooo" … my heart cried out like a wolf in pain. We were about twenty minutes from the Sawgrass Highway interchange. I yelled at Robin to pull over, as I was screaming and crying. Oh, my God, I thought. Everything had gone sour. My life, my soul had disappeared into vapors along with mom's dying body. Didn't anybody see?

We were the same, she and I. Mommy and baby. We were meant to be together. She wanted me so much. Did I do this? Did I wish this? Did she do this because of my own selfishness or did one of us have to go, and she was trying to save ME? A million crazy and unsubstantiated thoughts rallied through my head.

When we pulled up to the Manor Care Hospice, our tires screeching into the parking lot, Robin barely stopped to let me jump out. I ran blindly past all of the other patients and loved ones in the lobby, into her room. The Hospice nurse was standing outside like a statue awaiting my arrival. She had been crying. She took my hand and guided me into the room. I was not prepared for this. All I saw in the bed was an old, shriveled, dehydrated person, not the beautiful woman who I knew in life as my mother. She no longer was the Joan Crawford lookalike. She lay there lifeless and peaceful, and not my mother. No, it was not her, I kept telling myself. The part that was her was now inside of me.

As the nurse politely moved to the corner of the bed against the wall, she allowed me to have the courage to lean over and touch my mother's cool, waxy skin under the blankets. I wanted to get into the bed with her and shake her to life. Don't do this yet, Mom! I need a mother! I need you! These words were screaming inside my head, yet I couldn't utter a sound. The nurse hugged me tightly as we said our goodbyes and I thanked her for being the one person who was present as mom passed away.

I sat there in that room, ramrod straight in the hard hospital chair, staring at her form. In some small way, this gave me comfort to take in every bit of her while I still could. Her mouth was twisted into some kind of unsightly and strange shape and one tooth appeared to be overlapping her lip. In spite of all of this stark reality and the ugliness of physical death, I was calmed by her form and envisioned the angels who surrounded her with the golden glow of heaven who made her free and beautiful once again.

Long minutes passed as I sat there in total shock and stillness. I glanced over my right shoulder and noticed an elderly man who suddenly appeared near the next bed. Minutes before, his sickly wife was taken away briefly for some type of medical test. I didn't remember seeing him earlier.

As I looked at his frail form, he gave me a quick nod. I wasn't sure what it meant, but I took it as a recognition of my mom's death. I felt something else from him, something huge and comforting. I needed him to be there, even though we never spoke. I continued to look at him. His presence evoked a calm in me. I never figured out what transpired between us on that day, but I was grateful for him, nonetheless.

All I knew was that I was sitting in the room with my deceased mother, not knowing how I would continue to live my life. My whole body felt wracked inside and out and my heart felt like it lost its rhythm, although I knew I was alive in that room. That day, as I sat there with my mother's body, I realized that I needed to be there, looking at her, letting me know that life had changed for us both.

I felt a new defining moment in my life and a new appreciation for who my mother was, in every way. This wasn't the end of an era, but the beginning of a new one. A world of new opportunities and a chance to let the world know that I am here and I matter. I may have come into this world on a star that lost its way in the universe, but now that I've come full circle, I know who I am and that is good enough for now. I had two mothers and I was loved.

Saying Goodbye

I STOOD ALMOST lifeless in front of the kitchen window of my mom's condo as the black limousine approached us. I looked like hell from lack of sleep and the ever-present lack of my mother. As Robin and I made our way to the car that was going to take us to the cemetery, I was numb; however, I felt the eyes of my mom's neighbors looking over their catwalks wondering what was going on. Every one of them knew that it would be their turn to die, but yet hoping it wasn't today.

As I stared out the window of the limo holding back fifty-three years of tears, we drove to the Beth Israel Memorial site. When the car stopped, I ran to use the bathroom. I felt my insides churning and my face sweating in the sweltering South Florida heat. When I returned, I approached the car and looked over my left shoulder. There I saw her in the limousine. My mother was in a wooden box waiting to be thrown into the cold brown earth next to my dad. It hit me then: all the smells, the memories both good and bad, every last detail of her. The curvature of her face, how her thumb was badly bent and the beautiful golden Star of David that she always wore and would be buried with. I felt a rapid and strong wave of nausea overtake me as I lost my balance and leaned up against the car gasping for air, praying I wouldn't puke in front of the driver.

Robin steadied me with his body. We paused for a few seconds as we got back into the car and drove the three long minutes to the gravesite. My parent's plot was in a section called the "Book of Esther," with a gravestone that sloped into the earth, slightly lilting to one side, as it read, "Together Forever." At that precise moment, I knew this was the worst day of my life, and feared for what would come next.

Rabbi Brett walked over to console me as I saw Angel Mary, mom's caregiver, coming to the grave with Gloria, her employer, in tow. Here we were, a small group of people at my mom's grave, no other family and none of her friends. Most of them were either dead or too elderly to attend. I was burying her with very little fanfare, except for the birds who were singing above us. As the Rabbi uttered his prayers and said the perfunctory prayers for a Jewish funeral, I sobbed uncontrollably, flanked by Mary and Robin. I wanted so desperately to jump into that box and be with my mom one last time. I fought all of the urges to do so as the Rabbi continued to chant and pray in Hebrew.

At the precise moment that I went to throw my handful of dirt onto the casket, a huge gust of wind came by on one of the hottest days in June and blew all around us as it created a small whirling dervish. It was then that I felt her, if even for a brief second. I wanted to believe, but the feeling only lasted a moment and then it vanished, being replaced by a still shadow, motionless, quiet. Even the birds paused at that moment on a Tuesday morning.

As we departed for the limo, I suddenly remembered that I was born on a Tuesday, because Mom often said, "Tuesday's child is full of grace." I received an engraved gold necklace for my tenth birthday which bore that inscription. I have kept it tucked away all of these years. We both were connected by that day somehow. We had that. We were given that.

Once the ceremony was over, Rabbi Brett left us and wished us well, advising me that he would call later in the evening, which he did.

Mary remained with Robin and me for the entire day. I needed Mary desperately. She was the only person that had known first-hand what I had gone through these past few months, and I owed her everything.

Hours had gone by since the funeral, and it was approaching dark by the time I crawled my way into mom's double bed pretending I would see her in the morning. In my dreams, I waited for her. I guess, in a way, I'm still waiting …

The Lost Hand

AS I CONTINUED to mourn the death of my mother and her absence in my life, I came to the stark reality that I was beginning to suffer from a strange and debilitating malady. When did I see this second tragedy coming?

My husband, Robin, did and inquired over and over again for several weeks in the early fall of 2008, why my handwriting looked so sloppy and unfamiliar. Every time I signed a check at the grocery store he pointed out the distorted signature that was unfolding before his eyes. I must have been blind, as I never noticed or felt much. I do recall having the most beautiful and artistic cursive handwriting in grammar and middle school, and even in later years embarked on free enterprise and became a calligrapher of invitations and signs. I prided myself on this ability, the one artistic quality I possessed other than ballet dancing, and that was long over with, so my achy knees and bent toes tell me.

As the weeks went by, I began to feel "abnormal" from head to toe. My students whom I taught at Boca Ciega High School, noticed that my handwriting was significantly waning, as well as my speech. I was having difficulty holding the pen in my hand, and, due to loss of feeling, it felt like someone was tickling my hand so hard that I lost the grasp. Every single day that I tried to put the house key into the lock, I fumbled to excess, until finally the key ring landed on the back-porch steps with a heavy thud. Once again, all I felt was the whisper of a tickle.

All of these symptoms seemed to intensify during the first week of October in 2008, the very week that I took a short medical and personal leave from work to begin the daunting task of finalizing my mother's estate. I remember sitting at the computer writing my mother a letter as advised by my grief counselor, all the while bawling my eyes out, overcome with grief because she was not there to help me and she was never coming back. I wanted so much to tell her about these unusual symptoms. If only I could have picked up the phone and listened to her voice. She would understand. She would make it all better. After all, when I was a child, she gently and deliberately stroked my hands and fingers using great care as she applied the unique-smelling Pacquin's hand cream night after night. This was a long sought-after bedtime ritual that kept us close for at least twelve years.

As I sat at the computer that October morning, I could feel her hand on mine, the slightly scented cream floating around my nostrils. For several moments, I felt her warm breath on my neck and her presence surrounding me, as I pounded out the words to the letter. The lines of loss sunk deeper into my face, noticing them as I passed every mirror in the house. At the same time, the tingles and electric shock waves in my hand worsened day by day, and I bit my tongue repeatedly and uncontrollably. I often stopped to wonder, Am I suffering from PTSD due to the loss of my mom, or am I suffering from a dreaded and deadly disease? The symptoms continued to worsen, and both Robin and I worried more and more. I was becoming increasingly irritated during the day from lack of sleep due to the spasms in my right pinky toe, which had a mind of its own. Each and every evening starting around seven o'clock, my right pinky toe tapped into my other toes in a non-stop rhythm. When this first began, Robin and I laughed

about it over and over but it was not a laughing matter. The movements increased throughout the night, making an eight-hour's night
sleep impossible. The only saving grace was that there was no pain
involved. Eventually, my primary care physician sent me to a local St.
Petersburg neurologist who specialized in movement disorders and
was very successful with his patients. I had no choice but to seek his
medical attention.

I sat in Dr. Barnes' office and lamented on my hand, my impaired
speech, and my difficulty negotiating the stairs at home, not to mention
the lack of clarity in my head. I watched his face as he seemed to react
in a calm manner to what I was I saying. However, I occasionally observed a wary-eyed expression when he reacted to other symptoms that
I stated.

The next week I was out of school a day or two again for both a
cervical and brain MRI. I had to go miles from home to Rose
Radiology, a true "open MRI" establishment that kept me in an upright
position during the whole procedure, without the traditional enclo-
sures. My results came back within a week and Dr. Barnes reported on
a follow-up visit. "You have a normal neck for a woman your age,
along with some minor inflammation. There is nothing remarkable on
your brain which would indicate any tumors, malignancies, or abnor-
malities."

None of the reported findings resolved my dilemma. I was so relieved to know that I actually did have a brain after months of turmoil
since June and the summer that followed. Hearing the word "normal"
uttered from the doctor was a bonus.

In spite of the benign test results, the next six months continued
with more symptoms and maladies. I was having trouble piecing my
days together. I was sent for more tests locally and eventually con-
sented to a time-consuming and mentally grueling neuropsychiatric
evaluation. These groups of tests took its toll on me as I embarked on
its journey after school hours for several days in one week. By the time

seven o'clock in the evening rolled around, I was awake for seventeen long hours, had taught numerous classes at my high school, and was starved for food and adult conversation. Most of the tests consisted of memory recall, analogies both with words, numbers, and phrases and a myriad of abstract shapes that would make a geometry teacher scream with delight. I found out that it had the opposite effect on me.

About a week later, the psychologist, Dr. Rose, called to schedule a follow-up appointment to review my test results. What a daunting task that was. The actual complexity and rhythm of the tests had me realizing how brilliant I was in one area, and how mentally defective I was in another, but the results, once again, did not seem to disclose anything relevant to what I was suffering.

As months flew by, and I continued to struggle with all of the dropped glasses, limping legs, and slurred speech, I made another call in the hopes of getting more answers. On my own advice, in the early spring of 2010, I had secured an appointment with a Neurology specialist, Dr. Jay Van Gerpen, a renowned doctor and neuroscientist in the field of Parkinsonian and Movement Disorders at the world-famous Mayo Clinic in Jacksonville, Florida. Once again, I was forced to take a three-month medical leave from school, and we travelled up to North Florida with our little Shih-Tzu, Mia, in tow. Both Robin and I never had cause to seek out such an establishment until now. We were both amazed by its architectural beauty and grand scale of services that this facility provided. The buildings were surrounded by an enormous set of gardens and walking paths, all laid out so serenely to lend itself to the healing moment. I could have gotten lost there forever. I saw many people walking around with bald heads knowing their cancer battles within, but only from a distance.

Upon my first appointment, I was greeted by a friendly and open intake staff. They sent me an itinerary via the mail several weeks prior to my appointment and I was given specific directions to follow. The first day was spent being introduced to the neurologist and his staff.

As I watched him perform all kinds of minute tests that had great meaning, I watched as he wrote vigorously on his notepad, never missing a moment of my movements. Oh, how I envied him and his right hand as he was writing. At that moment, I became silently angry at the unknown. Why did my ailment show up at a time like this? He asked me all of the pertinent "first time" doctor visit questions, and my reply once again was, "I don't know, I was adopted."

It has been hard lying to doctors for all of these years, and it meant something important today to tell the truth. It meant how little I knew about my family. In fact, I knew almost nothing.

Dr. Van Gerpen mentioned how my condition had the good possibility of being a genetic disorder, but I was going to have to pursue that avenue on my own. I nodded, and we moved on with the exam. He watched as I attempted to draw with one hand and move the other hand in the air while my eyes were closed. Again, he took copious notes as my husband observed. Finally, after several hours of assessing the functions of my right hand and arm, he thanked me for being his patient. He told me that another MRI may be needed. However, when the look of fright appeared on my face, he dictated into the machine, "We will put the MRI on hold due to the patient's claustrophobia and anxiety." Thank you, Dr. Van Gerpen.

The next day, I was given a test to check for close to one hundred metals, poisons, and the like through multiple blood tests. As luck, would have it, that part was quick and painless and I was not the least upset. Robin and I had a quick break to grab a delightful breakfast in the upscale cafeteria and then it was back upstairs for a chest x-ray which was not very lengthy. With two out of the three days completed, Robin and I decided to venture to the beach for a while and spend some quality time with little Mia.

The last day of medical examination was the "mother lode" of neuropsychiatric evaluations. I really thought I was over this when I performed so poorly a month or so before. This was going to be the nail in the coffin, I thought.

I was introduced to the very congenial testing psychologist along with her staff and was given an interview. I remember pressing the issue of my mother's recent passing and letting the professionals know how grief stricken I was, all the while wondering if my confirmed complicated grief led me to this point. They did not seem impressed one way or the other with my answers and just kept plodding along. The psychologists were more concerned with how my brain reacted under stressful circumstances surrounding those tests. By the time the testing was completed, I could take no more of anything, not even the thought of a walk on the beach. I was completely spent. Robin and I were able to rest the remainder of the day and ate a lovely dinner at a superb Thai restaurant followed by a great night's sleep.

On the following morning, I was summoned for my last appointment with Dr. Van Gerpen. The bottom line, without spelling out all of the neuro-jargon, was that I had shown some minor improvement in a few essential areas of the tests compared to several months ago back home, but I had been given the diagnosis of "focal dystonia" which manifested itself in my hand and my ability to write. The layman terms for this diagnosis is "Writer's Cramp." As far as I was concerned, this was no cramp at all, but a bizarre cadre of symptoms generated by an unknown origin. The neurologist ended his report by summarily saying, "That I hope that this is not a harbinger of something to come such as a brain injury." Upon further evaluation of my MRI, it was reported that I had parietal atrophy, a degeneration of the parietal lobe of the brain, which plays an essential role in speech and many other life functions.

After receiving this diagnosis and being on a temporary disability leave from my teaching position, I was assigned to receive intensive physical and occupational therapy in St. Petersburg and was introduced to a knowledgeable and delightful hand therapist, Mina. She worked for a prominent group of orthopedic surgeons in the area, and was an expert in her field. After several hour-long sessions of observation and initial diagnosis, we began many different forms of treatment. It seemed to me at this point, that my right hand was not going to improve in its ability to write. The goal, however, was to allow my left hand to become totally functional for writing function, as well as gaining strength and flexibility. I met with the specialist three days a week and put my hand through rigorous stretches and exercises.

It was about halfway through our treatments, when Mina suggested that we try a special procedure, which I thought to be very unique and interesting as she presented it. This revolutionary technique was initially designed to help individuals such as post-war veterans, who had lost a limb in an attempt to help them regain the confidence and function they once had. Mina brought out a cardboard box that was a ten by ten inched square with a cutout on one side of the box. The box had a large mirror adhered to the left side of it facing outward. A piece of paper was placed inside the box under my right hand, as well as paper under my left hand. The goal was to look directly and only into the mirror, while drawing small circles and making small letters with my left hand. At the same time, I was to draw and write with the right hand inside the box. Using the reflective power of the mirror, I was "supposed" to see my hand writing, and assume it was my right hand doing all of the work. It was the strangest feeling that I had ever felt while writing, and in no way felt like a natural process. I honestly wasn't sure what the outcome was going to be, yet I continued to try it for several weeks, even going as far as having my own box made for home use. Somehow, my grand imagination and the extraordinary capabilities of my brain (yeah, right!) led me to figure it all out, and I lost sight of the original goal. At some point, it became apparent that I didn't care either way, and neither did my hand. I still was not writing.

As I approached the summer of 2013, the situation did not improve one bit. The only difference was that I was grateful that I didn't have a brain tumor or brain cancer, and that I could still function over-all. The harbinger that Dr. Van Gerpen talked about, fortunately did not come into play, but the bottom line was, that I had to make a de-cision that summer and put in for early retirement for my teaching job to be effective January 17, 2014. I knew this had to be done, as I could no longer keep up with the writing aspect, the grading of papers, and the fast pace it required to excel at my job, as I have always done for the past thirty-six years of a long-standing teaching career. As I look back in time, I realize that it was the only move to make, yet it still seems sad, as I loved my students and working with many teachers over the years.

As I write this memoir, I think of the overall physical pain that is still present in the continual striking of the keys for many hours each day, and know that something is still not right. I am sad that I can no longer use pretty stationary to write personal letters. I have missed out on all of those moments at the beach, when I get a great thought and cannot write it down.

I think about my mother with each and every page I write, and confirm to myself that her loss set off a chain of events in my body on the day she died. The one part of me other than my heart that she connected with the most, were my hands.

Mommy and me, hand in hand, every night for so many years; tenderly touching, connecting our hearts and spirits, not knowing what the future would bring for either of us. When I look down at my hands and apply my own lotion today, no longer using Pacquin's because it doesn't exist, I pray for my mom's healing touch on my lost hand.

Part Three
New Developments

Welcome to the Wolf Family
2013

FIFTY-EIGHT YEARS and many conversations later, having felt the pain of great loss along with secrets revealed, I learned that I was formally introduced to the Wolf family in the fall of 1955, around the time of the Jewish New Year, Rosh Hashanah. This confirmation came in the form of a small black and white photograph which was sent to me by one of my mother's few living cousins, Elaine, who currently resides in Massapequa, New York, a home I visited often as a young child.

I gingerly opened the long white envelope, bearing the familiar return address. My hands shook as I pulled out the preserved black and white photo with its zig-sag edges, and immediately saw myself. Robin, my husband of twenty-eight years, looked on with an expectant expression. He asked, "What's that?"

I replied with uncontrolled excitement, "Look, it's my birth announcement!"

As I held the photo in my sweaty hands, I was overcome by dizziness. My olfactory memory took over as I gently sniffed the small square picture, breathing in my mom's scent and everything that she was. The photo was titled "Happy New Year" and on the picture appeared my name, "I'm two months old and I'm now a member of the Wolf Family," which was clearly written in my mom's artistic handwriting. In the picture, I looked very tiny, but peaceful, sleeping on my side, adorned in a crocheted knit cap and sweater. My mouth was slightly parted and my cheeks were chubby for such a tiny infant. When I turned the picture over, it had my parent's address printed on it. I took a seat on the porch holding the precious baby picture to my chest, and couldn't let it go. My heart was beating so fast I could barely take a breath. The best part of my evening was just beginning in lieu of this new find.

Elaine had been present at my father's funeral in 1997, and I had spoken with her on many occasions after my mother's passing in 2008, in an attempt to let family members know the agony of my loss. I wrote her a long letter in 2011 asking for clarification of my adoption, along with the usual chit-chat. She replied back soon after with many stories of our family on my mom's side including things that she thought were pertinent. I am not sure if it was due to fear, laziness, or regret that I never responded to her pleadings for me to call her. It took this last letter from her, dated January 13, 2013, accompanied by the birth announcement, to gather the courage to talk with her on the phone that very night. Out of the blue with no time to think, Elaine asked me if I wanted to know where I came from. I eagerly replied, "Yes!" as I paced nervously back and forth on the porch floor, my heart pumping fiercely in my chest. Her answer took me by surprise, as it wasn't half as exciting as what I had expected, awaiting the story of a lifetime. Yet Elaine reaffirmed for me the long-awaited truth in such a matter of fact way that I was surprised after all. She had partially answered the "who" question in my lifelong search, or so I thought.

I have often wondered why I am so driven to find this woman, my birth mother. My friends are convinced that it is no longer important, but more of a curiosity. No, my dearest friends, it is more complex than that. It is the primordial connection, once again coming into play. I have no real intense longing from love to meet with my birth mother, as I have never wanted or loved another mother than the one who cared for me my whole life. In fact, I craved the only mother I knew for many years, but we faltered in so many ways. The connection wasn't always there, no matter how much I loved her in life and always will in every way possible.

Elaine continued on about how one of my mother's cousins, who was Elaine's uncle, Abraham Cohen, was a doctor in New York City on the Upper East Side. If one knows this area of New York, only the upper echelon of people resides there. The real estate prices alone would cause you to cringe.

As she recalls the tale, back in 1955, a lone young woman patient who was obviously pregnant and of some financial stature, had an affair with an unknown gentleman, of whom I have yet to inquire. There it was, the beginnings of me! Consequently, I was named Nanette Beth Wolf, born on a Tuesday, on a hot July day in 1955. My mother always said, "Tuesday's child is full of grace." As I later researched my name, I found out that Nanette is actually a name with multiple meanings, such as "favor, grace, mystic, teacher, philosopher, quiet, and introspective." I am not sure if I lived up to those monikers. Maybe one day I'll find out.

Elaine and I talked for about an hour after that confession, and it set my head and heart whirling in many different directions. *Is she still alive?* I wondered without voicing the question aloud. Elaine volunteered that she believed my birth father was no longer living but did not volunteer any more details than that, and I ran out of courage to probe further on the matter. However, the question still remains, "what prompted her to give me up for adoption and what were her true circumstances?" Maybe I will never know the answer to that question in my lifetime, but I certainly would like to have that opportunity to learn, however it comes about.

Identity Crisis
2014

IT WAS COUSIN Elaine who inspired me to make inquiries into my identity.

In October 2014, I referenced The Adoption Registry of the State of New York website. The purpose of this agency was to help registered participants receive information about their birth families. They made it very clear that they did not foster reunions.

As I sat at my desk, staring at the printed papers, I cried. I couldn't believe that my existence had boiled down to a Google search. It proved evident to me that I had no rights as an adopted child. It seemed that my birth-mother was given all of the rights and power. Why should she or the State be the ones to choose if I knew my origins or not? I felt angry.

I reflected again on the stories I heard about how I got here, and it all seemed so surreal. No stories appeared to match. I was determined to get to the bottom of it. I owed myself answers. Many questions still plagued me after all of these years.

Why didn't my parents want me to know I was adopted?

Who were my parents protecting?

Were my birth parents Jewish?

Who were my cousins protecting?

Were they protecting my mother?

When I filled out the first form, I was asked if I wanted identifying or non-identifying information. I paused to think about it.

Identifying, of course. It's a no-brainer. I wanted to know the names, ages and physical features of my birth parents. More questions flew through my head.

Did my birth mother have my green eyes?

Was she a bookworm like me?

Did she ever suffer from back and neck issues?

Did she have dystonia, a genetic disorder?

Was she in love with the man who was my father?

I stared down at the form. I checked the non-identifying information box. I was scared. Scared of what it would reveal. That's all there was to it. I answered a few simple questions about my name, address, phone number, mother's maiden name, and place of birth. The form was notarized and mailed to the adoption registry via certified mail.

Several months later, I received an envelope with the return address of The State of New York Adoption Registry. I tore it open. It was signed by the Adoption Registry Manager, and he responded by saying:

"Your application to the New York State Department of Health Adoption and Medical Information Registry was received. The Adoption registry is authorized to release certain information to adoptees who were born and/or adopted in New York State. As soon as the Registry verifies that you were both born and adopted in New York State, you will be sent notice of your registration and your **registry identification number**. This may take several months, but please be assured the Registry is processing your request and will contact you as soon as possible."

The letter also stated that I would need to send a copy of my birth certificate.

I stared down at the paper. My hands shook. More tears fell. I wanted to vomit. What liars they are, I thought. They already know who I am. They issued my original and fake birth certificate. My name is part of the mega database of Vital Statistics. Why won't they tell me the truth? I felt like a number, having no human qualities. They were strongly reinforcing my lack of confidence in being adopted.

I inhaled deeply and dropped the paper on the floor. I was left with a profound sense of disappointment and loneliness. I was not important enough to be found.

It took several days to recover, but I mailed them another request along with the birth certificate they required. What else could I do?

After months with no answers, I received another letter signed by the Adoption Registry Manager on July 6, 2015, one day after my sixtieth birthday. The people at the agency reiterated that they do not handle reunions or find birth parents.

You've got to be kidding me, I thought. These people are sitting in front of my file, and cannot give me information.

I was still angry. I read the letter which said:

"Enclosed is the available non-identifying information about your birth parents and your adoption. The New York State Department of Health Adoption and Registry obtained this information from your original birth certificate, the records of the court, and the agency (if any) that handled your adoption." I scanned the letter for any pertinent information or names of my parents. Nothing.

The letter continued, "There are many situations where non-identifying information is rather limited. Therefore, the records will have little or no information."

Fuck you, State of New York.

I was given a new name as of August 21, 2015. I am #156-55-424931. That is my registry number from the State. I contemplated getting a tattoo, a constant reminder of the only true identity I knew. I declined.

The correspondence responded to my third plea for information. It now updated my file from Non-Identifying to Identifying. The letter informed me that I am registered for life, but that I will not be given information unless a birthparent or sibling has voluntarily registered.

I was held hostage by a family whose DNA I shared, but never met.

As the days went by, searching became my full-time job. I continued to scour the website for additional information. I realized that the adoption registry also sponsored a database for birth relatives who were searching for the adoptee as well. The database was arranged by year. Red represented female and blue for male.

I continued to scroll down looking for my birthdate. I stopped scrolling when I saw the birthdate, 6/5/55. So close. I continued down the page. I realized that there was no guarantee that this was my real birthday. More questions.

I believed that I was sixty-two years old, but what if I was only fifty-nine?

Is it possible that the birthdate was wrong and someone made a mistake?

I continued to read every word for every adoptee. I read for three hours in one day. The next birthdate in summer appeared as August 20, 1955. Not a chance.

I searched another column. A few birth mother names caught my eye. Agnes O'Reilly. She sounded Irish, I looked Irish. It wasn't her. Her daughter was found.

After hours of computer searching, I no longer could take the stress. My eyes saw only a big blur of names. I felt heartbroken.

In May of 2017, I received another envelope bearing a return address from the Surrogate's Court, Queens County, New York. Feeling hopeful, I opened the envelope slowly and read the note and accompanying information sheet. The letter read as follows:

"I am responding to your request for a certificate of Adoption and Petition to Access Sealed Records. I have searched our files for your adoption proceeding and have not found it listed in the records of this court."

I looked down at the notice and my fists balled up. I felt the bile rise in my throat. It felt like I couldn't breathe.

The information revealed the following information:
My parents were married.
My birth mom was twenty-four years old.
My birthfather was twenty-six.
Both my parents were Caucasian and born in the United States.
My father was a self-employed builder.

No other identifying information was found.

The letter read, "Your father abandoned your mother within months of your birth. He was a self-employed builder."

There it was. Abandoned by my birth father. What a way to start a life. I tried to think of the mother that I didn't know. She was young, most likely without a job, depending upon her husband. He could build a home but not a family.

As I continued down the page, I found that I was born at 4:21 AM and was five and a half pounds. My birth was normal without any complication for myself or my birthmother. The information revealed that my parents had no other children prior to my birth. My birthmother voluntarily put me up for adoption. The birthfather walked away without staking any claim to me, or standing up for his wife.

Coward.

Learning More
2018

IT WASN'T EVEN a few weeks after I wrote a letter to Governor Cuomo, asking him for the gift of my identity, that I received a reply in mid-April. I stared at the linen-white envelope embossed with the return address which read: The State of New York Executive Chamber, Albany, New York. I was shocked that it arrived so soon. I quickly glossed over the letter and noticed the unrecognizable signature of Governor Andrew Cuomo. The ink was still fresh on the paper. I don't know why I did it, but I sniffed the letter as if doing so would reveal a long-awaited truth.

The letter summed up by saying that the Honorable Governor understood my plight and would refer my case to the proper employee in his Executive Chamber. More political rantings from a politician who knows little about these matters. Although I researched some of his causes earlier last year and found out that he did support revision of the bill that would allow adoptees to own their own lives. At least I found a sympathizer.

After I read the letter, I filed it away in a special red folder that was reserved for all government papers which held any biological information about me. One day, I hope to throw it all away as a sign of successful reclamation of who I am. I wish that I would have been able to share this with my mother, as I felt she would be very proud of me for pursuing what I held most dear.

A few days went by and I received another letter, this one bearing the address of a Robert LoCicero, Director of the Bureau of Vital Statistics for New York. He basically reiterated what Governor Cuomo had said, but with a slight tone of, "you went over my head with this." I gave it a short look anyway, and just as I was about to move it to the red file, I noticed that the last line said to call him directly at his office if I had any further questions.

On Friday, April twenty-seventh, I called his office and left a message with his secretary who assured me that he would return my call as soon as he was available. I didn't feel hopeful. But the following Monday afternoon, while dining at a local eatery, I received a call with the area code 518. I thought to myself in two seconds, could this be LoCicero? Yes, it was. Our conversation went something like this:

"Good afternoon, Is this Nanette Davis?"

"Yes," I replied, my heart beating wildly. "Who is this?" I knew at this point, but wanted to make sure.

"This is Robert LoCicero, Director of Bureau Statistics."

He seemed to have a pleasant voice, young maybe. I waited.

"How can I help you?" he asked.

He knew how, I thought, but I took a deep breath and I continued along.

"I know you are aware that I contacted Governor Cuomo with my request to unseal my adoption papers and reveal my original birth certificate."

He said, "Yes."

He asked me what my goals were.

"I want to find my birth parents, particularly my mother. I want to know more about them and contact them."

"Do you have any particular reasons for wanting to know them?" he asked.

"It is my right to do so, sir, but more than that, I want to look in the face of the brave woman who gave birth to me. I want to thank her. I want her to know me, and offer my help to her. I want a mother now. I want to know why I have dystonia, and my hand doesn't work. I want to know why I'm having all of these maladies for the past several years."

I stopped to take a breather. I was standing in a portico of a public place. Several people paused to ask if I was alright. I nodded yes. And breathed again. He encouraged me to continue and I lamented on a few more of my thoughts.

Then he said, "Do you have any relatives who can give you answers?"

I replied, "No." I quickly gave him the ten-second version from cousin Elaine, whom I was going to see in late spring.

He kept responding by saying, "uh-huh, right, okay."

I felt a genuine feeling from this man. I felt that he was listening to me and trying to do something, if only for a moment.

After our twenty-five-minute conversation, he said, "We are getting ready to revisit this bill that we have been talking about. We are hopeful that in the next few months, we can resolve it for all New York adoptees. However, at this point, there is still a law, and I am bound to uphold it."

Blah, blah, blah. Suddenly, I didn't want to hear him anymore.

Then he added, "But I have a suggestion to make and you should do this first."

I asked him what it was.

He said, "Sue the State of New York."

I wanted to ask him, are you fucking crazy? I knew better. But he kept going.

"When are you going to be in NY next?"

"August, as part of our vacation."

He said, "Great. Secure a representative here and ask to get on the docket for the Supreme Court, and ask for your records to be unsealed. You'll get them."

"Without a lawyer?"

"Yes."

I stood there, exhausted and elated. This was the most concrete information someone in government has given me about my adoption.

As we exchanged a few niceties, he said, "So, in 1963, when you were adopted ..." Whaat, what, wait a min ... I thought. I froze and didn't ask a thing.

He finished his sentence.

" ... Things were difficult. We'll be in touch. Please call if I can help you any further. Good luck to you. Stay strong," he said.

"Thank you so very much again," I said.

I pressed the red button on my i-phone and ended the call. I collapsed into a small chair in the portico.

There, I did it. I was haunted by the "1963" comment. Could he have made a mistake? Did he mean 1953? A difference of two years I could handle, but ten? No, I'm older than 52.

I put the phone back into my purse, opened the door to the café, sat down and finished my grilled feta with avocado.

The year 1963 remained on my mind. I couldn't handle another secret.

Too Hot to Handle

IT'S BEEN SEVERAL months since I've spoken with Governor Cuomo and weeks since I've been advised to go to the Supreme Court in New York City. Hope was in the air and I followed all of the State's instructions to secure my original birth certificate. My God-given birthright.

When I consulted with a local Florida law firm, the woman who took my information was impressed. Ms. Carlton of the Carlton law firm said, "Mrs. Davis, you've done an extraordinary job of researching. Most people who are searching (she never mentioned for what, but used the word like it was part of a lingo related to adoptees), come to us starting from the very beginning. You obviously have been working on this for some time."

I nodded and continued by saying, "This all started after my mom passed away, as I had great reservation about hurting her feelings while she was still alive."

"That's understandable," Ms. Carlton said, "but it can be a difficult process regardless of the situation."

She perused my paperwork, and looked up at me and frowned when she said, "Unfortunately, we cannot take an adoption case in Florida when the adoptee hails from New York, but I can refer you to an attorney in Albany. His name is Edwin Baldwin and he specializes in Adoption Law. At the very least, he can give you good direction."

I felt disappointed at her response, but it made sense. Every state is independent in this matter. If I *was* born in Florida, I would have been well on my way to knowing who I was and when I was born.

The next day I called the attorney whom she recommended and I left a detailed message on his message service. He returned my call the next day. We spoke for a brief moment in which he said, "Nanette, I've listened to your message and I don't believe that I can help you. For one, I practice in Albany, and you need to work with someone who was from your county of birth and according to what you said, it would be Queens."

"Wait, Mr. Baldwin, I said, "I wrote to Governor Cuomo and he claimed that he would assist me in this matter. Mr. LoCicero told me to sue the state of New York. He said I didn't need a lawyer, but I just wanted someone to get the court paperwork in order. You know, a representative."

He quickly responded by saying," Ms. Davis, I can't help you, but I will give you these other names."

"Please," I pleaded with him. I started to rant on and on about how I may have found my birth parents through an obituary, making an assumption that the man was a self-employed builder and that he would have been the right age. In addition, his wife was deceased, but it started to make sense. I am still researching the prospect of these people who were married in Greenbush, New York, a small town near Albany. I continue on about how Robert LoCicero said that if I followed his recommendations, I would be successful.

It was at that very moment where he appeared agitated and forcefully said, "That's enough, I can't listen anymore. You're giving me too much information, we are going to have to end this call."

I was spittin' nails but I shut up. Just as I was about to say, "thanks anyway," he hung up. But, before he did, he left me with another contact, a female adoption attorney out of New York City. Her name was Roberta Fagan. I called her the next day, and waited at least one week. My phone call was never returned. I guess that speaks volumes about my "touchy" case. I guess I'm too hot to handle.

Doc Cohen

AS I TIPTOED down the creaky wood stairs of Cousin Elaine's
living room, I caught a glimpse of his face. It was the man who held
me in his arms hours before I was turned over to my adoptive parents.
I edged closer to the coffee table and picked up the gilded-framed
photo and stared at it. I ran my hands over the smooth glass and closed
my eyes imagining how he felt. It was "Doc" Abraham Cohen and his
wife Dorothy, Elaine's aunt and uncle. I breathed in the dusty odor of
the framed picture and put it to my heart. I felt the connection immediately. Maybe it was because he was the only one who looked into my
birth-mother's eyes and heard her voice and reassured her that I would
be okay. I wish he wasn't dead. I wish I could ask him one question.
Who was she?

I visualized days long gone spent in Tarrytown, New York, where
Doc was born. My memory led me down a path of warmth and safety,
surrounded by people who loved me. Doc arranged my adoption in
1955, but I haven't seen a photograph of him in more than thirty years.
I haven't spoken with him since I was ten years old, before I even knew
I was on this adoption journey.

I opened my eyes and stared hard at his face. His skin looked
smooth and he seemed happy and kind. After all, he assisted my

adoptive parents in realizing their dream. My mom's dream. I wondered what it was like for him to speak with my birth mother, a newly married young woman, whose husband abandoned her. She must have been terrified. I wondered when my birth mother came to Doc's office as a patient, as Elaine's story goes.

I gave a thought as to what my grandparents were like and felt for a small moment that I missed them, even though I never met either of them.

The shame of divorce in 1955 was surpassed by the shame of giving up your one and only child. Only that notion changed on June 27, 2018.

Elaine and I were having lunch in her kitchen and we were sharing photos when she said, "Nanette, something just crossed my mind." I leaned in closer. "I don't know if I should tell you this, but I heard from my mother many years ago that there was another child born to your birth mother."

I stared at her in disbelief. I retorted, "Elaine, that's impossible. The state paper, the state paper." I waved it in front of her face. "It says right here." I pointed to the lines that clearly stated that there were no other children prior to my birth.

Elaine looked into her lap. I looked down at her kitchen floor and counted the blue tiles. I waited for her to continue speaking. She did not. I felt confused, disgusted, and disappointed all at once. The whole situation was getting ridiculous in a hurry. It seems that great lengths have been taken to keep me separated from my birth mother and father. I, Nanette Wolf Davis, still remain parts unknown.

Conversations with a Ghost

IT WAS SEVERAL days after I arrived home from my visit with Elaine that I received an email from her dinner guest, Beatrice Newman. We had a short conversation at Elaine's dinner table which centered around my adoption story. She had seemed to take an interest in me. I almost felt like I had met her before, but from where I couldn't place. I knew that Elaine spent a good deal of time with Beatrice. She owned her own company in Manhattan and was connected to many people. So was her husband, Sal.

The email referenced her desire to help me in my search, not by doing it herself, but by recommending someone who had conducted searches for a long time and had a big voice in the adoption community. Her name was Evelyn Larkin, and she was an adoptee as well. Apparently, Evelyn is an adoption rights activist and had lobbied Congress for many years on behalf of thousands of New York adoptees.

I dialed her number and left a message, after a Google search to make sure she was legit. Even though she was recommended by Beatrice, I felt a need to find out some more information about her. The internet turned up nothing more than a website that sounded more like a business for handmade craft items. I wanted to make sure that I was talking with someone who wasn't out there for the purpose of hacking my information.

Her recorded message sounded pleasant, and I gave her the shortened version of my story and how I was referred. She called me back within twenty minutes and we had a short but pinpointed conversation.

"Nanette Davis?" She inquired.

"Yes, is this Evelyn?" I could see her called ID on my phone.

"What can I help you with? Beatrice told me a little about your adoption story. But, before I ask you too many questions, let me tell you about myself. I'm an adoptee and even though I was told about my adoption much earlier on, I did not know my birth parents. That part was kept secret as well. I was born in New York, but live elsewhere now. I was able to meet my birth parents and have a relationship with them.

She did not mention where she lived and I didn't ask.

"I'm an adoption rights activist as well, and have been involved in helping to change the adoption laws for many years in New York. It has been a tough battle, but it has to be done. The Governor did approve a bill to move forward in our favor, but it is going to take more than a year before it gets the votes."

I listened to her but was starting to feel that it was going to be a duplicate of my other inquiries with the state.

"I want to petition the court for my adoption records, Evelyn, but I am not sure how to do this." I explained the whole conversation that I had previously with the state officials. This is getting very complicated but I am willing to try anything at this point. I had planned on having a court date by August when we are in New York for a week on vacation."

It seemed like time was running out, and the court appearance wasn't going to happen.

"What are your parents' names? Where were you born? Did you have any adoptive siblings? How did you learn about your adoption?"

All of these questions and many more came in rapid fire, as if she was writing the information down, or possibly recording my voice. I could hear children playing in the background, and I assumed they belonged to her.

"I just came back from a conference, so I am trying to unpack and return to normal. You know how that is."

"I wanted to let you know, Evelyn, that it was Dr. Abraham Cohen who arranged my adoption. He was Elaine's cousin. My birth mother was supposedly a patient of his as well as her parents."

"Hmmmm," she said. "I think I have heard that name, Dr. Cohen. He may have been part of a larger adoption network. Yes, I think I have heard that."

I felt like we weren't really getting anywhere and that I was repeating the same information to everyone I had spoken to without any new results. It was frustrating to say the least.

I asked her if she thought that I had a chance to petition the court in New York when I was there and let her know I was going to call the court again.

She replied by saying, "I want to introduce you to someone who can give you a better legal argument for your petition. You will not be able to use the medical argument for your dystonia condition. The bill does not allow for that as a main reason for reunion. I know this sounds crazy."

I was dumbfounded.

"So, what if I am going to die from dystonia? Doesn't that mean anything?"

She became quiet and listened to me cry a bit.

"Ok, Nanette, let me get in touch with my contact in New York, and do some more follow-up on Abraham Cohen. I'll get back to you in a few days. Is that okay?"

"It'll have to be," I said.

With those words, we said our goodbyes. I hung up the phone and lowered myself into my worn-out comfy chair and sobbed. I waved my husband away as he tried to ask about the conversation. I really didn't know *who* I was talking with, and the continual lack of action got the best of me. I decided to put it to bed for the night and read instead to take my mind off things for a while.

When I awoke early the next morning, I checked my email and there was a message from Evelyn to a Gregory Leuce, a well-known adoption rights attorney in New York. The email stated:

"Greg, this is Nanette who is looking to petition the court for her birth records. She is an adoptee and has an interesting story. You may be able to help her."

And then she added, "Nanette, it may be a good idea for you to wait until you have more legal information before processing your documents. That would be my suggestion. I hope this works out for you."

There it was. A cryptic email from Evelyn introducing me to another person whom I've never met. Five days went by with no other phone calls, emails, or outreaches. I felt like I spoke with a ghost. I felt like I could have my identity at my fingertips, only to be let go in a matter of minutes.

The veil of uncertainty grows deeper in my search for my birth family. I am, at this point, still a persona non-grata and feel myself wanting to give up the fight.

The New York Vortex

I TOOK A trip to New York on August 4, 2018 to try once again to secure my identity. After several conversations with New York officials days earlier, I had my doubts. But my husband and I flew out anyway, in hopes of a fun time coupled with the business of finding myself.

The day after we arrived, on a steamy, hot, and oppressive morning, we ventured to Long Island to introduce my husband, Robin, to Cousin Elaine for the first time. It was the highlight of the trip, as I watched Robin interact with Elaine and her extended family. Both of us were glad that we took the opportunity to do this, as it further solidified our family bond.

The next day we got up early and walked the two blocks to the infamous main branch of the New York Public Library. We showed up promptly, when they first opened, and eagerly awaited my appointment with someone in the Genealogy Department.

When I approached the desk, and asked the studious looking gentleman about the process to view the New York birth index, I was nervous. My palms sweated. I felt my heart pound in my chest. This could be the moment of my reveal. I leaned in and introduced myself to him.

"Good morning, I have an appointment to work with a genealogist today. My name, well, my name that I think I have, is Nanette Beth Wolf. On my fake birth certificate, it is listed as Nanette Beth Wolf Davis, as I am now married." I pointed to my husband, Robin, who smiled and nodded.

"Good morning," the genealogist replied. I didn't catch his name right away. "Here, let me show you to the genealogy computers, and you can get started. The birth index runs from 1916-1965. Is that what you want?"

"Yes, thank you." My hands still shook. I felt he was watching me closely. I gazed around the room with its grand and beautiful wood fixtures, holding clues to real people who lived at one time or another. I breathed in the scent of the old books and took delight in it. I was surrounded by comfort, by history. I grew up around old people, and I felt secure in this old room, filled with relics and old books. I felt connected somehow to all of it. Maybe it was because I knew that room held my identity somewhere. I was determined to find it.

I snapped myself out of my thoughts and heard the gentleman say, "Mrs. Davis, this is how you browse through the history. May I see your current birth certificate or any papers that you have?" I handed him the small certificate along with information from New York State.

"I'm going to the Supreme Court tomorrow to petition for my adoption records and original birth certificate. I'm unrepresented and this process has been quite a task."

He smiled and then said, "I wish you the best of luck, but I tell you it is not an easy process in this state. Maybe you will have luck with the registry. Some people who have done this do not need to go any further and find what they want right here." He pointed to the image that showed up on the screen.

"Let's first look under the name you were given. That would-be Nanette Beth Wolf. Is, that, right? Birth certificate number 143-29-5689."

"Yes." He typed in "page 773" which revealed names starting with the letter W. As he scrolled down the page, I saw all of the people who were born in 1955 in New York. All of the boroughs were represented and it was amazing. He stopped at Wolf. I scanned down as did he. No Nanette Wolf. No female Wolf. No evidence of me.

Tears started to well up. He turned to me and said, "Mrs. Davis, you can't necessarily go by the name. It is the year and the number that matters the most. In cases like yours, people go to great lengths to change the names, so as not to be found. I'm sure you're already aware of this."

I nodded.

"Unfortunately, you will have to go through hundreds of numbers, possibly thousands, starting from the beginning. It will take a long time. No one can do it in one sitting. Why don't you spend some time now and then come back on another day? If you need any more help, please ask. Good luck." His voice was gentle and kind. I'm sure he had to deal with people's emotions on a regular basis. He smiled and returned to his desk. I thanked him for his time.

In spite of the fact that I spent over six hours in two days perusing the birth index, regardless of what the name started with, I felt that I was touching something important. I felt that I was in this record somewhere, but time would only tell when I would discover it.

As I sat there exhausted, with Robin dozing alongside me in another chair, I figured I could check Mom's name and see if she appeared on the list. I scrolled down to Bressler and it didn't take long, only two entries, and there she was. Bressler, Harriet S, born on December 15. It was good to see her name. It made everything more real for me. I took a picture of it with my phone and ran my hand along the name, as if to seal it.

The next day, Robin and I were up early, and hit the transportation trail. It was difficult to want to dress nicely when the temperature outside was soaring and smog filled the air. We grabbed the bus on

Seventh Avenue, which headed downtown to the Court district on Centre Street. We boarded the bus and made our way to the back where seating was more available. We could have taken the subway, but I refused due to the heat factor. This was going to take some time, but it was worth it considering what I might find out.

A woman sat in the very back of the bus by herself. She was pleasant looking and smiled at us when we sat down. She seemed to be enjoying herself and in no particular hurry to go anywhere. After about twenty minutes, we became confused as to the stop we needed to get off at. It was hard to read all of the street signs.

Without us asking her, she leaned over and said, "Good morning, where do you need to go?" I guess we had that "are we there yet?" look on our faces.

"We're headed to the Supreme Court on Centre Street. Do we get off at that stop?"

"No," she replied. "You want Duane Street. It is a good connector. You'll have to walk several blocks, but you will see all of the federal buildings. You'll know you are there by the amount of Homeland Security vehicles."

As we approached our stop, she said, "It's going to be a longer trip going back as the traffic will be slower. The off-peak schedule may give you longer wait times. I'm not sure what your schedule is, but good luck anyway." As I pulled the cord to signal the bus driver that we wanted to get off, I turned around and thanked her for the directions.

Robin said to her, "You're an angel, and we appreciate all you did to research the stops."

"My name is Angelica. I wish you a good trip."

Wow, I thought as we got off of the bus, she was an angel. Most people would have not spoken or even offered. It wasn't like we asked her for help. She just volunteered it. Hmmm, interesting. Was it an omen?

Angelica was right. We walked the seven blocks toward the courthouse, seeing men and women scurrying with briefcases, wiping their sweaty brows from the mid-morning sun. I could see the thick columns of the New York State Supreme Court looming tall and impressive as we rounded the corner. We stood there for a few minutes and glanced all around, taking in the magnitude of this building. I thought of all the people who were trying to change their lives or circumstances. This building represented much more than law. This building represented freedom or in some cases the hope of freedom. I couldn't believe that I was here and asking for my identity. I started to cry and sat down on the steps. I turned to Robin and said, "I don't know if I can do this or if I should do this."

He smiled at me and reassured me it was going to be OK. Words have power most of the time, but the word "OK" didn't feel big enough. I wasn't convinced. But, I was here and was willing to give it a try.

We passed through the security aisle, emptying our bags and assuring the officers that we were not a threat. I asked the woman where Room 119 was located. This was the room where unrepresented people go when they are filing a motion themselves. In my case, I was going to sue the State of New York for my adoption records and original birth certificate. I was going to be the plaintiff. That word sounded funny. I said it again to myself, plaintiff. The State was the defendant. This was a far cry from a *Law and Order* case, and I was entering the big leagues with nothing more than a beggar's note and a warm smile.

As I approached a middle-aged gentleman who was the Clerk of the Court, I glanced around and realized it was just a room. No judge, jury, or any of the usual findings in a courtroom. My shoulders relaxed a bit.

The man stepped forward and asked, "How can I help you?"

"I'm Nanette Beth Wolf Davis and I'm here unrepresented to petition the court for my adoption records. I already called and we flew in from Florida several days ago. I have paperwork from the State. I have a letter from Renee Collins of the New York Surrogate Court who told me that my records were not found in the State Court system." I felt like I was already losing control and wanted to ramble on. *Steady, girl.*

The gentleman asked me many questions over and over. He looked through coke bottle glasses, and I couldn't see his eyes to tell if he was lying to me. An elderly man appeared from a closed room and walked slowly toward the front of the desk area. He sat down on a stool. He didn't speak; he just listened. He was large and frail at the same time, but with a kind face. He smiled at me and listened to everything the clerk said. He watched me intensely and I wondered why he was there. No one else seemed to pay attention to him or even recognize that he was there. What was his role?

I kept looking at him and couldn't stop staring. The only thing I knew is that he calmed me down. My hands stopped shaking and my thoughts came together. He somehow made me ready to answer the clerk's questions.

"Let me see your paperwork. What do you have there? Where are your files located? Have you located in what district your records are housed?" He kept firing away.

"Sir, I want to petition the court for my adoption records. I spoke with Renee Collins," I continued to repeat myself.

"I know, I know," the clerk said as he looked over his glasses at me. "But, where was your adoption filed?"

If I knew that I wouldn't be here. "I don't know," I said. "This is all that I have. See, my parents were married. See, I have a letter from Governor Cuomo. LoCicero said to come here." I was already exhausted and getting nowhere.

During this time, I knew he was listening and taking in every word. Contrary to what it seemed, I was being looked out for, but in the way that *they* do things. Shut up and listen, I said to myself.

Before Robin and I left the office, the clerk handed me a large stack of papers stapled together and said, "Ms. Davis, you seem determined to pursue this to the end. You seem like you know what you want to do. Given that, I'm saying to you, take these papers and read them over carefully. We suggest hiring an attorney. Even though you are unrepresented now, it might make it easier. You need to get a long-form birth certificate. Do you have one of those?"

"No, only the small rectangular paper, but it has a seal."

"That won't work. You need to go to across the street to the Vital Statistics Building. Ask them for your long form record of birth. If they can produce it, we are moving in the right direction. There is a small fee, but that paper is important. Call the Help Center noted on the paperwork if you run into any technical problems."

He looked over his glasses and said, "I don't have to tell you what your odds are, do I?"

"No, sir, I already know, but that doesn't matter."

The older man nodded and smiled again. "Have a nice day," he said.

We left the room, and I managed to make it to the large wooden bench near the door before the river of tears ran down my face. My heart was heavy. Years of believing one thing, finding out something different, and feeling like one big experiment gone wrong was too much to bear. Before I realized what was happening, several people of different ages walked toward our direction at a leisurely stride. Some hovered, some sat. No one said anything. Robin saw them too. They were lawyer-types but less formal in their dress. They sat there while I sobbed and did nothing more than smile. I was confused by their presence, but at the same time, relaxed.

A few minutes had passed when I collected myself, and Robin and I headed toward the elevators. I was in desperate need of tissues and cold water on my face. A pleasant looking, nicely dressed black woman appeared at the moment I asked Robin about the bathroom location.

I know it seemed odd, but true. She just appeared. Without me asking her a single word, she came over and caught my attention by putting up her hand and waving toward the elevator.

And then she spoke.

"The woman's restroom is up one floor and then around the corner and then down these stairs. It's very odd and unusual."

"Uh, what's unusual about it?" I asked. I was getting a strange feeling. I never solicited her help.

"C'mon, let me show you." Into the elevator we went. She chatted more about the odd staircase. Suddenly, I felt that I was in a Harry Potter movie. Robin just listened.

When we got off the elevator, I looked all around and took in the beauty of the building. I looked down and saw a rotunda with historical pieces, and it took me back to a simpler time. One without cell phones, distractions, and where no one needed an adoption unsealed. I relished in the moment.

The woman pointed toward the ceiling, and said with a smile again, "There, dear, up those stairs, then down a set of stairs. You'll find it. Have a wonderful day."

As I turned to say "thank you," she had turned and walked away. No goodbyes, just gone.

The staircase was an experience in and of itself, and held an allure of the original courthouse, with massive granite steps and wooden banisters. Once in the restroom, I looked into the mirror and splashed some water on my face, trying to contain the mascara that was caked under my eyes and on my cheeks. "Hi, Nanette," I said. "One day, I'll find you."

I tossed the paper towels into the trashcan, situated my backpack on my shoulders, pressed my shoulder blades together to straighten my posture, and walked up the stairs back to Robin.

With a somewhat renewed physical state, Robin and I headed over to the Vital Statistics Building. We were greeted with blasts of hot air, as the whole building lost their air conditioning due to the extreme temperatures that had put pressure on the New York power grid.

"Whew!" I said as we entered the revolving doors.

"Please step forward, ma'am." The security personnel motioned us forward.

"What's with your a/c in here?"

"Please open your bags, folks." I could tell they were all business.

We entered the room for certificates. At least thirty people were on line in the close quarters. This was a different group of people than in the courthouse, and many customers did not refrain from using foul language or any such gestures. Various security personnel stood like armed statues in the corners of the room, awaiting any possibility of a fight which could break out at any moment. I waited almost thirty minutes until it was my turn to face the clerk.

I studied her as I said, "Good morning, I was sent over here by the Supreme Court Clerk to see if I can secure my long form birth certificate, uh, my amended birth certificate." I remembered I was advised not to use the word "fake," as it sounded inflammatory.

"Where you born in New York? In Queens?" *She already knew.*

"Yes. But I need the long form certificate. I was adopted in 1955. I am trying to see if you have that record of birth."

She nodded that she understood.

I watched her face intently as she stared at a computer screen. I felt like a dog salivating for food that was being held in a hand, but at arm's length. If only I could reach under the glass and turn that computer around. I imagined what I would see. Names, descriptions, addresses, possibly pictures of my family that I was born into. If only I had a million dollars, I would hand it to her and say;

"Here, have a good life, now please, I beg you, give me back mine." *If only.*

I looked up when she said, "Here it is, long form. Make a copy if you wish, and keep it in a safe place."

"No adoption record to go with it?" I said, halfway joking.

"No, I'm sorry, ma'am, we just do certificates. Have a nice day."

She was looking beyond my head as the line grew by the minute.

"Thank you."

Robin and I walked out of the crowded room and found an un-occupied corner to stand. As putrid as the building smelled, from all of the worn-out and sweaty bodies, I wanted to look at my long form sheet. It was the closest thing that I had to normalcy. I needed that now.

For that one moment in time, surrounded by the cacophony of sounds around me, everything became quiet. When I looked down at my parents' typewritten names, my heart and mind joined together. I saw my parents' signatures on the bottom of the paper. If only for a matter of seconds, I closed my eyes and visualized my parents signing this form. It was a moment like no other. I heard my mom's voice as clear as if she was whispering in my ear. Hers was joyful, beautiful. I saw her beautiful face and she was smiling. This was *her* moment that she waited for all of her life. I uttered aloud in the quiet, dream-like moment, "I love you, Mom. I love you and I thank you."

I opened my eyes and we were still standing in the same spot. As we made our way to the entrance of the building, many faces turned in our direction. They all had looks of contentment. They seemed happy. Maybe some of those strangers along the way shared my story. I glanced at the people of all sizes, shapes, ages, and wondered about their life story. I wondered if I could be related to any of them, but a passing glance or a smile could never reveal any truths, only stir the imagination. *If only.* I put the thought to bed and the next thing I knew we were searching for the bus back to Madison Avenue. I was tired and longed for a cold shower and a cold drink.

As we headed down Centre Street towards Broome Street, we passed the New York Family Courthouse. Dozens of children of all ages with their siblings and parents were coming in and out. I wondered why they were there. *Were they the center of custody battles, divorces, foster care placement, or even adoptions?*

I spotted a New York police officer sitting at a desk inside of the building. He appeared to be chatting with an employee.

"Robin, let's go ask this officer for directions back to Madison. Maybe there's a shorter route. No way am I going in the subway. Too damn hot."

He nodded in agreement.

The officer had a beautiful smile. Tanned skin, shocking blue eyes, shaved head, wearing a bullet-proof vest. He looked like a movie star. We approached the desk to ask him about the M20 bus.

"Can I help you?" he asked in a most pleasant voice. *That smile again.*

"Good afternoon, sir. We're looking for the bus that goes down Madison Avenue. We just came from the Supreme Court, but we're a little bit turned around right now. Heat's got us."

He laughed and said, "The Supreme Court. What's going on there?"

A few employees meandered over. We got their attention.

"Oh, I'm trying to get my adoption records, uh, here." I pulled out my manila envelope with the stack of papers.

A few more people came by and just leaned on the counter.

He looked more closely at them and put on his reading glasses.

"Why do ya need the Supreme Court? Family court is where you want to be. That's where family matters take place, adoptions, etc."

I gave him the Governor Cuomo lowdown report.

"Cuomo! That guy's a bum!" he said.

Robin looked over at me with raised eyebrows.

"He held me hostage," I said.

"Why did he hold you hostage?" *Odd question, considering he called him a bum two seconds before. Steady girl. This guy has got dirt. Too sweet though.*

"He won't release the records. You know, court laws and all. But my Cousin Elaine in Massapequa, she's ninety-three this week, she's been helping me," I rambled on.

"Massapequa? Where in Massapequa?"

I gave him the address and her full name. Then I leaned in closer, gave a quick look around and whispered, "Did you know that the Gambino bosses, Joey Buttafucco and all of these mobsters lived there? Some still do. In these *huge* homes?"

He laughed and said, "Yeah, what do ya want, it's Massapequa. I think I know your aunt, cousin or whatevah. I'm her neighbah. Lake side of the street, right?"

"Yes, oh, wow, I can't believe it."

I could not believe that out of all the millions of people in New York City, I stumbled upon a police offer who was my cousin's neighbor, AND, of all places, in a family court. This was just too much for coincidence.

The police officer must have realized why we were really there, and said, "Don't take the bus. The subway is right around the cornah."

A slew of directions followed. Then he stood up, shook both of our hands, and said, "Have a safe trip back home."

Out the door we went, back to the hotel. What a day! Robin and I were exhausted. When we fell into bed that night, I listened to Robin snore. I laid awake for several hours and thought about our downtown courtroom adventure. I realized that this was the beginning of something big. I tried to make sense out of the connections we made with people who were pure strangers, yet I felt strongly connected to them. I had to admit, that even with my skepticism, that every person we met played a part in my journey. Not just a face, or a voice, but an unseen delicate hand placed on mine, to lead me to the truth. I had become part of the New York Vortex.

Musings from the Heart

I HAVE COME to the realization that my life will never be the same. I am forever changed. Changed by death. Changed by time. It is an incomprehensible thought that I have to say or read these words. They come out of my mouth, but they sound wrong. The intellectual me says, "This is not possible. My mother promised me she would never die."

I say the words, "My mother died on June 16, 2008 at 12:20 p.m."

I say them again. This time louder, as if it would help me understand.

"My mother died on June 16, 2008." I scream these words, but my heart refuses to believe it.

Like a young child, I believed her, even in the midst of her last year of life. I have been forced to watch the woman who made my life a reality fifty-three years ago die.

Life is very complicated for me right now. I do not feel like I am a part of the present. Yet, I don't know what the future will feel like. The past is too painful. I feel like I am living with a veil of uncertainty each and every day. I try to sort out the feelings, but, some days, I am not sure what a feeling is, or how I am supposed to capture it.

All I ever wanted in life was for my mom and me to be together. I wanted to be the most special person in her life, and, of course, I wanted her to be mine. After all, she made my life possible after birth.

For some reasons that I can't explain, I have always been afraid that I would lose her. I mourned her death even as a young girl. That was an awful place to be.

It was true that I had been a difficult teenager, more than most. I did stupid things, some that were dishonorable, some that I would be too ashamed to mention. I tried to reconcile why I behaved badly, but I always knew that I didn't do anything to cause intentional pain or hurt to anyone in my family.

I admit that I was tired and lost and confused all at once.

Simply put, I had a love affair with my mother. No, not in the way that one would be horrified to think about, but in the way that you act when you feel you could never get enough of someone wonderful.

For a long time, when I was able to understand many of my feelings, I labeled myself crazy, abnormal, needy, unstable. I finally found out that this was not the case.

Shortly after Mom died, I read a book titled "The Primal Wound" by Nancy Verrier. This book saved my life. It let me know that I was not unstable or crazy, but was adopted as a very young infant. My adoption came with a price. The price of trauma. What do I mean by that?

In her book, Nancy Verrier discusses the premise of being separated from the birth mother and the trauma that follows. She states in another book, "Coming Home to Self," that "I believe that being separated from the original mother is a trauma, the ultimate loss and rejection, and an experience which has life-long consequences for both mother and child."

She continues, "This trauma has been ignored because we, as a society, have deluded ourselves into believing that adoption has little or no effect on children, and therefore, does not have to be addressed as a way of understanding these children's feeling and behaviors."

I read this book frantically from cover to cover and discovered ME. I cried as I read and realized there was a true and verified reason for some of the behaviors I displayed both as a child and in my adult life. I was looking at myself in a mirror on every page. I have always questioned my thoughts, attitudes, behaviors, and views of the world. I wondered why I felt so alienated even when relationships seemed perfect. Issues of abandonment, a current theme in my life, have explanations which I share with thousands of other people, some whom I know quite well.

It seems as if my brain searches for a center, without having an original starting point. That made so much sense to me, as I have not learned of my origins.

Because I spent so many years very numb and exhausted from trying so hard to fit in, I didn't act fast enough when Mom truly needed me. She was not good at expressing her feelings, and I needed her to say what was on her mind. I needed her to tell me that I was the dutiful daughter, that I needed to step up my game. After my father died, my confusion was strong, and I paid little attention to her small pleas for help. In unraveling my own grief over him, I saw how lonely she became, but didn't grasp the full extent of it.

As she came closer to death, I pretended that it was not final. I put off feeling as long as possible, so that I could deal with everyday occurrences.

I waited for her to tell me all of my life that I was hers. I waited to for her to tell me that I was a loving daughter and that I was pretty and she was proud. I waited and waited for more than fifty years. But, the point was, she did tell me, with her birthday trails, keeping every card I sent her and articles about school. Every single day. I didn't listen or maybe I didn't hear.

It wasn't until I couldn't touch her anymore, that I believed every single word she said. For once in my life, I felt the real love that a mother has for a child. I felt the real love that she had for ME. In that moment, I was not an orphan. I belonged. The hole that had been in my heart for many, many years had begun to miraculously close.

Every so often in the wee hours of the night, and sleep doesn't come, I put my hand on my heart and say "I love you, Mom. I've always loved you."

Finding the Family that I Once Knew

I HAD MADE two visits in recent months to Cousin Elaine and her family. Both times, the food was tasty, the conversation even better. But what really stood out for me was the re-connection to a family that I already had. Sometimes you look real hard for something in your life, and it doesn't always pan out the way you wanted it to. As a result, you make choices. That's what I did.

Years ago, I made the choice to leave New York, knowing that my family was there. I made the choice to run away to faraway places to avoid conflict and confrontation. I had to live with those choices of alienation, because adoption can sometimes teach us that, if we're not fully grounded.

The conversations that I have had with Elaine in the past five years have left me with a renewed sense of family that I didn't see before. Through the eyes of an elderly and brave woman who, through losing her sister at an early age to suicide, and a husband to Alzheimer's, still showed the brighter side of herself on any given day. From the moment that she became aware that I was on the rocky road of pursuing my birth parents' identity she supported me, and gave me reasons to reflect on my life. She told me she loved me a hundred times and looked forward to hearing my voice when I called. There were many times in my life that I felt less than, both physically and mentally, but Elaine had her way of squelching my hurt, and letting me see my own worthiness. One that I always questioned.

Elaine would end our phone conversations about my identity search with, "I think you are doing the right thing. I believe that everyone should know where they come from."

"I think you're great," Elaine insisted time and time again. "You were such a beautiful baby and an adorable child. You always looked so cute in your little white outfit with the red piping."

I replied, "Thank you, but I hated that hat. It looked like a flying saucer and the elastic strap cut my neck."

Elaine and my mother were very similar and became good friends as well as cousins. Elaine saw first-hand the struggles my mother went through as a young adult, and was there for her during many times in her life. My mother would be thrilled that Elaine and I have reconnected. She would have seen Elaine as a loving mother figure for me since she is gone. She never held judgement, she just gave love.

The love that unfolded at Elaine's dinner table, on both occasions I visited, was obvious through all of the quirky remarks exchanged between Elaine and her son, Richard. They had a special bond, one that I always longed for in my own life, but that never materialized.

Richard called his mother by her first name, and it made me laugh.

"Elaine, let Robin and Nanette eat, they've already heard that story."

Elaine pursed her lips in a half smile, and said, "And he called his father the old man." We all chuckled.

As we sat around the lunch table, we munched on son-in-law Brad's chef-inspired meal of gourmet sandwiches and baba ganoush. In between chomps of lettuce wraps and pieces of bread fit for a king, dipped in olive tapenade, we rehashed family war stories, as we laughed non-stop.

"Do you remember the house in Tarrytown, and the stairs to the second floor?" I asked Elaine. "That house was horrible."

Elaine stopped to think and replied, "Poor Andy had to live upstairs in that tiny apartment. They were all crammed into that house."

She shook her head at the memory.

"Andy's first wife was a real bimbo. I can't remember her name," I added.

"Oh, speaking of Andy, you're in the will." Richard nodded to Elaine.

We all laughed. It must have been a family joke. I paused for a moment to think, what will?

I could see the family unit, and the love for Elaine's grandchildren, as well as her granddaughter's husband, and it is real. Despite the usual ups and downs of family living, there is a thread of security that runs deep in this family, and everyone knows they are in this world together, helping each other in good times and bad.

On the day that Robin and I went to see Elaine, I kept looking at the clock on her kitchen wall, nervous that we would miss the train. The truth was that I wished I never had to leave her, as she was going to celebrate her ninety-third birthday in a few days. I hoped it wouldn't be her last. As we stood up from the large dining room table that has seen many family dinners such as this one, I kissed Elaine, her son, and daughter-in-law, Kathy.

Elaine looked like she was getting ready to cry as I hugged her, and she said, "I wish you would stay, but I know you have plans in the city. Please come back soon, and of course, you too, Robin," and she gestured in his direction.

I looked at Robin and he was beaming. My heart burst at the acceptance and the love that he must have felt at that moment.

I leaned over to Elaine and said aloud, "You're the only family I have."

Richard smiled, and Elaine's home health aide, Nadia, had tears well up in her eyes. It was a tender moment for everyone.

Kathy looked up at me and said "Awwww." I'm sure many thoughts were going through everyone's head.

As we were dozing to the clickety-clack of the train headed back to the city, I realized how our visit gave me a new perspective in my search for my birthparents. Even though the recurrent anger at being an adopted child and treated like a second-class citizen flares up late at night, I feel now that I am better equipped to take on what is rightfully mine. My birthright. I realized how lucky I was. I did have family. I always had. Sometimes it wasn't perfect, but what family is? If I am not successful in my quest, however prevalent in my life it has become, I will breathe and know that I have family, and they are still here.

Part Four
Tributes to Mom

Homage to Mom
2008

MOMMY, I MISS you so very much. I see all of the middle-aged women having lunch with their mothers. They are doing things with them, and I can't be with you. I feel so alone. It makes me sad that we are not together.

I came into this world in 1955. Twenty-two years later, I pushed you away from me and I don't know why. I missed out on all of those years that we could have been sharing and holding hands, and going places. I still can't believe that you are gone. How come I can't see you? Will I ever see you? I keep torturing myself over the fact that we won't share more good times.

Sometimes I feel you as if you are right here with me, yet the reality of it is, we won't be going to lunch. We won't be talking on the phone.

I am lost Mom, truly lost. I hope that you are thinking of me every day.

There isn't a day that goes by that I don't miss our three o'clock chats on the phone.

I always wanted someone to tell my woes to, and you were right there all along … and for so many years.

I missed what was right in front of me. I can't get you out of my head. I never want you out of my heart.

I will try again tomorrow.

I love you Mom.

Forgiveness
2009

AS I MULLED over some of my childhood experiences I saw what a strange and unique child I was.

Could it be possible that the woman who gave birth to me on that July day knew what she was going to have to encounter with me in her life? Did her intuition prevent her from keeping me?

As I search for answers to this perpetual question, I think about how I approached life. Many of my secrets are screaming to be told yet I am so worried about how my friends and family would perceive me. I am sorry for so many things.

I am sorry …

For the coins that I stole from your drawer, Daddy.

For the times that I told you that I hated you, Mommy.

For running away in elementary school and hiding by the railroad just so you would feel bad. I tried to get back at you so that you would spend more time with me.

For using drugs when I was a teenager and stealing Nanny's barbiturates to escape my horrible days.

For lying and falsifying a note saying that I was very sick and couldn't come to work at the mall when I was seventeen years old.

For running away from home when I was eighteen and making you wonder what happened to me.

For seeing you standing outside of Lynn's house on the corner looking like your whole world had been crushed.

For being late for our Mother's Day special dinner when I was twenty-one and you thought I wasn't coming.

For not being with you the whole night after Daddy died.

For not calling you often enough until it got too late.

Things I am not sorry for …

For

For …

Letter to Mom
June 16, 2009

DEAR MOM,

I am writing this letter to let you know so many things. I am preparing myself to honor your first anniversary in heaven, as you left this world. I can't believe that it was a year ago today. It was the hardest moment of my life to get that phone call as Robin and I were driving on the highway. I knew who was calling when I answered my phone. I really hoped that I would be there at the exact moment that you died, so I could hold you and hope that you weren't scared. I don't know if you saw or knew that I was in the room with you, just a little bit after you passed away. I waited until the Hospice nurse left. I just wanted it to be the two of us.

I couldn't believe how it didn't look like you at all. I really wanted to stay holding your hand, but it seemed uncomfortable to do. I was surprised that I wasn't scared to be alone with you. I had anticipated that I would be. You know how I was afraid at funerals. I honestly felt like you were right there with me, only not in the way you looked in the bed. I felt intensely guilty because I wanted your suffering to end so badly, that weeks before I prayed that you would be taken and relieved of your pain. I hope that you weren't upset with me for thinking that, but I just wanted all of your loneliness to disappear and to be with the rest of your family eternally.

I often wonder where you are right now. There is a part of me that wants to be right where you are. Are you a beam of light? Or a star in the universe? I'm sure that you are the brightest star in the cold, dark, blackness of space. I imagine a luminous glow all around your head.

I want you to know Mommy, I believed everything that you said to me the last few months before you died.

I remember when you said, "Nanette, you are the best daughter I ever had." I always replied, "Mom, I'm your only daughter." When I said that you would laugh a little and say. "Oh, silly."

I replied the way I did time after time, because I was emphasizing the fact that I was your daughter. Your special daughter. Given to you. We had some really great conversations, didn't we? Sometimes I didn't know if you understood what I was saying. But, I looked forward to our three o'clock phone calls. Conversations were short sometimes. Hearing your voice made things a lot better.

Then one day, early in the morning, I called you on the way home from a typical Saturday gym workout. It wasn't typical at all. You didn't answer the phone. I called at least ten times. I was frantic and knew that something was wrong. I could feel you inside of my heart, calling me and letting me know that you were in trouble.

I finally pulled the car over on a side street and screamed out the window, "Mommy, Mommy, answer the phone." Oh, my God, Mommy! I shrieked. I felt myself getting nauseous, and my hands were shaking so hard, I had trouble holding the phone. The song, "In the Arms of an Angel, by Sarah McLaughlin was playing on the CD player, and it was fueling my outbursts of sadness and hysteria.

I drove home speeding all the way. I didn't care if a cop pulled me over. I ran out of the car and into the back door of the house, still screaming for you. Mrs. Wadley, our neighbor next door came over to the fence to see if I was alright. I couldn't catch my breath, and tried to tell her you weren't answering the phone, but I couldn't get the words out.

Finally, I managed to tell Robin what happened when I called you and he calmly told me to call a local hospital. I wanted to call but I was too scared. Scared that the nurses would say that you were dead. I wasn't ready at that moment to hear those words, even though I knew you had suffered.

My thoughts immediately turned to Mary, your caregiver, and I knew that she would know what was happening. When I dialed her number and she answered after four long rings, I told her that you were not answering the phone. She sounded upset, but offered to drive over and check on you, even though it was her day off. She called me back fifteen minutes later and found the door busted down and the window screen was broken as well as the window. Mary said she would call the police. She asked me to hold tight, and minutes later, the Delray Beach Police called me. They explained that it was the fire department who busted down your door, as you fell and managed to crawl to your phone in the living room near the big glass table, and ask for help. Mom, that took incredible courage, as you could have just lied there and called it quits. I'm glad you didn't, as it gave us more time that we both needed.

I was terrified, Mom, but I managed to hold it together. The police said that you were in bad shape but conscious and took you to Delray Medical Center on the sixth floor. I called the hospital right away and when I finally heard your voice, I screamed at you. Can you believe that? I screamed at you because I was mad that you didn't call ME! I was mad that I wasn't the first person who you would call. I screamed because I had no one to help me with what was going on. No sister, or brother, or anyone who was family.

After I spoke to the nurse in charge, she told me how you were injured. I cried during our whole conversation. I told you that we were coming the next day and would be there early in the morning. Robin and I walked into the hospital room, and the first words that flew out of my mouth were, "Mom, you look a fright." I couldn't believe that I said that to you. But you agreed with me. It was the first time, Mom, that I was looking at you and didn't recognize you.

I remember walking over to the charge nurse and saying, "My mom is going to Hospice." She replied, "that's impossible, she is not Hospice material." Five hours later, Robin and I wheeled you into the Pinecrest Hospice Unit of Delray Medical. That began your final journey.

Prologue to Mom's 8th Grade Essay: "I Grow Up" 2003

TIME IS FLEETING away now. My mother is getting older. Her needs are changing and so is mine. As I watch her struggle with life at eighty-five years old, and what it means to her, so do I.

I feel the need to surround myself with her presence like never before. I can do this even if she is two hundred miles away. I have begun the process of loving her for who she once was, and appreciating all that she is now. I see now all that she gave to this world, and all of the things she will continue to give.

After forty-five years, I have never known her as well as I do now. As I look through her pictures and memorabilia, her writings and stories, I gather a new insight into what it was like to be Harriet Sybil Bressler, my mother.

I came upon this essay, entitled, "I Grow Up," in a rather roundabout way. The essay was written in 1929, when my mother was in the eighth grade. She spoke very little to me about her life as a child, maybe it was because she had been living as someone else, not ever coming to grips with her real soul. I wept as I read these papers, all torn and tattered, with the aroma of her childhood still intact. In truth, I know that her struggles were mine, and feeling her humanity has grown her closer to me.

She cannot leave this world without me telling her this.

Mom's greatest desire in life was to write something that people would remember, and something that was truly great. Well, Mom, you did write something great.

This is a gift to you, Mother, on your eighty-fifth birthday, to help fulfill your lifelong dream.

… I love you …

June 16th 2018
Gratitude

I'VE FORGOTTEN HOW beautiful the beach makes me feel. With each lap of the surf or squawk of a seagull, I'm surrounded by the love that Mother nature provides me.

Today, I return to the exact spot where ten years ago when I sat on a bench, faced the sea and asked YOU to take my mother. I prayed for her release from her pain. I prayed for return of my sanity. I asked for forgiveness, even if I didn't need it. I closed my eyes and let all of nature swallow me in its gentle blanket of love. I was grateful.

Ten years later …

I add a new piece to this peaceful moment. I release each helium balloon filled with little messages to my adoptive mother. Messages of hope. Messages of relief. Messages of love. I'm letting go of my angst and all the resentment that I've harbored for years.

I'm letting go of the idea that I didn't care for my mother and some of the lies that I told myself. I'm letting go so that she can smile and feel peace, knowing that I am and will be okay.

I'm letting go and touching my heart and feeling love all around me.

An ever-present love for Mother Nature, my adoptive mother, my birth mother and the mother deep inside me that I would have been.

Where I'm From: A Reflection
2019

I'm from Long Island
Where the prize-winning roses
And the scent of Mom's Tabu
Fills the air.

Family birthday parties occupy
The big lawn and Hawaiian Punch flows
Like water.

Auntie Claire simmers her favorite liver and onions
On the outdoor skillet,
As we take turns winning at Candyland
Reminding ourselves of who cheats best.

Nanny fills our ears with stories of the Great Subway Robbery
While Aunt Mickey smokes her corn cob pipe,
Puff! Puff! Puff!

Photo Gallery

The Wooden Shoe, Present Day

Mom and Nanette

Nanette Age 5

Nanette as an Infant

Asheville, NC

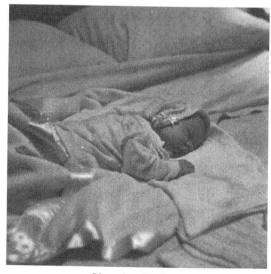

Sleeping Infant

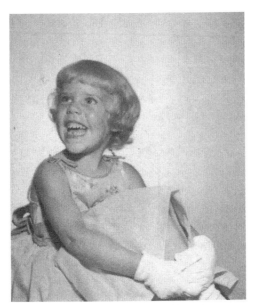

Birthday Dress-up; Age 4

Nanette at Grandma Eva's House

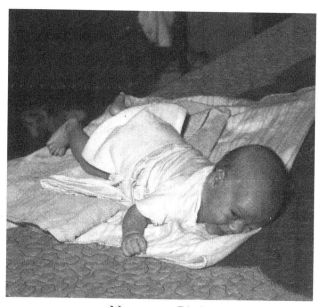

Nanette at Birth

Letters

Dear Mom,

I chose this poem for you on Mother Day because it expresses the true feelings of love on Mothers Day.

This poem is one of my favorites by my favorite romantic poet. John Keats.

A Thing of Beauty
John Keats

A thing of beauty is a joy forever:
Its loveliness increases; It will never
Pass into nothingness; but still will keep
A bower quiet for us, and a sleep
Full of sweet dreams, and health, and quiet
                breathing.
Therefore, on every morrow, are we wreathing
A flowery band to bind us to the earth,
Spite of despondence, of the inhuman dearth
Of noble natures, of the gloomy days,
Of all the unhealthy and o'er darkened ways
Made for our searching: yes, in spite of all,
Some shape of beauty moves away the pall
From our dark spirits. Such the sun, the moon,

Trees old and young, sprouting a shady boon
For simple sheep; and such are daffodils
With the green world they live in; and
clear rills
That for themselves a cooling covert made
'Gainst the hot season; the mid-forest brake,
Rich with a sprinkling of fair musk-rose
blooms:
And such too is the grandeur of the dooms
We have imagined for the mighty dead;
All lovely tales that we have heard
or read,
An endless fountain of immortal
drink,
Pouring unto us from heaven's brink.

Oct 17, 1997

Dearest Nanette,

Your phone call the other
morning made my day. I
wish we could make the calls
more often – it makes me
feel closer – we have a lot of
lost time to make up. Did
I ever tell you how much I
love you? (to infinity!!)

Keeping busy – looks like
rain this afternoon so I'm going
to the movies with my friend
Florence Holt and probably grab a
bite afterwards. Tomorrow I'm
going to see a show with Bobbie +
her cousins. Supposed to be a

comedy (Grandma Sara's Funeral!!)
I'll let you know!!!
    Thats all for now. Love
to Robert.   I love you!
            Mother

Dearest Nanette,

It seems as if I'm looking around and everywhere there is just nothing. The contact between us seems so superficial— we are just mouthings because its the thing to do— "I love you I love you"— so what does that mean beyond the words on the telephone? You have made a life— I'm happy that it seems to have turned out so well in spite of all obstacles both real and created. Where does that leave me?— There is just no room for me there— I must create my own life here such as it is. I have all the right ingredients but one— ME. I just can't get over the feeling of always being on the fringes- neither here nor there. I'm like divided between here & there & feeling

as if I don't belong anywhere! The
Mens Club is having a holiday program &
I can't find anyone to go with me. I
guess I'll have to go it alone — well I
can't have someone holding my hand all the
time & I have to stop running away from the
world. Here goes!

Don't be frightened — I'm
just letting off steam & mailing it
before I chicken out! Love you!

Dearest Nanette

    I can't begin to
tell you how much
your visit meant to
me.

    Called you last nite
but didn't seem to get
through — very frustrating.
Can you try to tell me
when & how we can talk?
    Love to Robert
        Love
          Mother

Newspaper Article

Parents

Adoption cuts all ties to children

The Charlotte (N.C.) Observer recently ran a feature about a 41-year-old Charlotte woman who became pregnant while she was a teen-ager and unmarried, and gave up her first child for adoption.

Her story wrenched the heart. She was herself adopted. She was placed in a home for unwed mothers, and eventually persuaded to give up her baby.

Twenty-four years later, at the urging of a psychotherapist, she went looking for her long-lost son. With the help of a search consultant, she found him, called and announced, "I'm your mother."

The young man, a quadriplegic since an auto accident at age 16, met with her. They have established a relationship and she has asked him to come live with her.

"It just doesn't go away," she says of the longing she carried with her for 24 years.

The article was greatly disturbing to me.

I feel tremendous compassion for a 16-year-old girl who had no choice other than to give up her baby. I feel tremendous compassion for that same woman who, 24 years later, still grieves over the loss of her first-born.

Nevertheless, I feel an injustice has been done.

John Rosemond is a family psychologist in private practice in North Carolina.

trude into their lives saying to their son, "I'm your mother."

The story raises several important questions:

Q. Who are the parents of an adopted child?

A. An adopted child has one set of parents, and they are the two individuals who accepted and carried out the daily responsibilities of raising him. Giving birth does not necessarily a parent make.

Q. Does a parent who gives up a child for adoption have a right to find and contact that child years later, much less attempt to "reclaim" him?

A. Absolutely not. Once an adoption is final, parental rights cease forever.

It may not be illegal to go looking, years later, for your adopted offspring, but it is unethical.

It is self-serving and can only disrupt the life of the child and his family, and that is something no one has a right to do, regardless of the circumstances of the adoption.

Q. Is it proper for a therapist to encourage a grieving person to look for his or her adopted offspring?

A. Again, no. Therapists should offer support and help these people work through their grief, but they should never act as the catalyst to an event that has the potential of bringing emotional chaos into the lives of innocent people.

As I said, I feel for the woman.

But even though she is now capable of giving her offspring a loving, stable home, that doesn't alter the fact that as a teen-ager, she was probably not capable, emotionally or otherwise, of doing so.

The story should have been balanced with views from the "other side."

On the one hand, there's the hurt of giving up a child.

But on the other, there's the hurt of adopting and raising that child only to have someone suddenly intrude into your life.

Birthday Card

July 5, 1971

Diary for the Day:
Today was my Birthday
In the morning I opened
up my fantastic presents.
Then my mom & dad
took me to see 1776 which
was ultra - fabulous.
At night we went to
the Park Inn for dinner
which I thought was
very nice. Afterwards
Cindy came to the house.
All in all, it was the
best birthday I ever
had!! Thanks —

There are lots
of special wishes
In this Birthday book
for you
Because today you're
SWEET SIXTEEN
And very lovely, too;
May you be very happy
As future years unfold
In recalling all
the memories
This little book will hold

$65.00 from
July 4 -
party with
relatives

Remembrances:
Gifts I got -
Mother + Father:
1) Baby Bracelet
2) Ruby Earrings
3) Sweet "16" charm
4) James Taylor record
5) Hot pants outfit
16 pennies 16 nickels 16 dimes
Friend's gifts
Heart Earrings
Ruby Earrings
Jewelry Box

3 glorious days
Weather was nice

Darling Nanette
"How much do I love
thee.
Let me count the ways"
It was a wonderful day
to remember. May all your
birthdays be as happy
Love
Mother

PASTE
PICTURE
HERE

Birthday Wishes

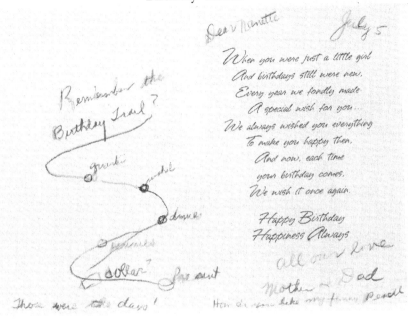

Note to Mom

My Speech
I think that I should
not be punished until
next Monday. I think
that Wen. is too little
time to start. I therorr
I would like to say that
you should wait until
the proper time which
is next week.
  The punishment days
  will be as follows:
MONDAY to THURSDAY.
      Thank You.
      Miss nanette Wol

Dear Mother
I love you
very much.

49310798R00127

Made in the USA
San Bernardino, CA
21 August 2019